THOSE WHO LIVE IN GLASS HOUSES

DRAMA

Kraftgriots

Also in the series (DRAMA)

Rasheed Gbadamosi: *Trees Grow in the Desert*
Rasheed Gbadamosi: *3 Plays*
Akomaye Oko: *The Cynic*
Chris Nwamuo: *The Squeeze & Other Plays*
Olu Obafemi: *Naira Has No Gender*
Chinyere Okafor: *Campus Palavar & Other Plays*
Chinyere Okafor: *The Lion and the Iroko*
Ahmed Yerima: *The Silent Gods*
Ebereonwu: *Cobweb Seduction*
Ahmed Yerima: *Kaffir's Last Game*
Ahmed Yerima: *The Bishop & the Soul* with *Thank You Lord*
Ahmed Yerima: *The Trials of Oba Ovonramwen*
Ahmed Yerima: *Attahiru*
Ahmed Yerima: *The Sick People* (2000)
Omome Anao: *Lions at War & Other Plays* (2000)
Ahmed Yerima: *Dry Leaves on Ukan Trees* (2001)
Ahmed Yerima: *The Sisters* (2001)
Niyi Osundare: *The State Visit* (2002)
Ahmed Yerima: *Yemoja* (2002)
Ahmed Yerima: *The Lottery Ticket* (2002)
Muritala Sule: *Wetie* (2003)
Ahmed Yerima: *Otaelo* (2003)
Ahmed Yerima: *The Angel & Other Plays* (2004)
Ahmed Yerima: *The Limam & Ade Ire* (2004)
Onyebuchi Nwosu: *Bleeding Scars* (2005)
Ahmed Yerima: *Ameh Oboni the Great* (2006)
Femi Osofisan: *Fiddlers on a Midnight Lark* (2006)
Ahmed Yerima: *Hard Ground* (2006), winner, The Nigeria Prize for
    Literature, 2006 and winner, ANA/NDDC J.P. Clark Drama Prize, 2006
Ahmed Yerima: *Idemili* (2006)
Ahmed Yerima: *Erelu-Kuti* (2006)
Austine E. Anigala: *Cold Wings of Darkness* (2006)
Austine E. Anigala: *The Living Dead* (2006)
Felix A. Akinsipe: *Never and Never* (2006)
Ahmed Yerima: *Aetu* (2007)
Chukwuma Anyanwu: *Boundless Love* (2007)
Ben Binebai: *Corpers' Verdict* (2007)
John Iwuh: *The Village Lamb* (2007), winner, ANA/NDDC J.P. Clark
    Drama Prize, 2008
Chris Anyokwu: *Ufuoma* (2007)
Ahmed Yerima: *The Wives* (2007)

THOSE WHO LIVE IN GLASS HOUSES

DRAMA

Obii Okwelume

kraftgriots

Published by

Kraft Books Limited
6A Polytechnic Road, Sango, Ibadan
Box 22084, University of Ibadan Post Office
Ibadan, Oyo State, Nigeria
☎ +234 (0)803 348 2474, +234 (0)805 129 1191
E-mail: kraftbooks@yahoo.com;
kraftbookslimited@gmail.com
Website: www.kraftbookslimited.com

First published 2016

ISBN 978–978–918–355–5

= KRAFTGRIOTS =
(A literary imprint of Kraft Books Limited)

First printing, February 2016

For Furofa

Other titles by the Author

Three Plays
Ogurigwe (A Play)
Arrow of Vengeance
Babel of Voices (A Nigerian Satire)
Drumbeats of Black Africa: A Collection of African Proverbs

Contents

The plays contained in this volume are works of fiction. References to real people, events, places, establishments and organisations are used fictitiously.

Those Who Live in Glass Houses

July, 2014

Characters

<table>
<tr><td>KOKORI</td><td>—</td><td>Abiama chairman</td></tr>
<tr><td>EBITI</td><td>—</td><td>Kokori's political associate</td></tr>
<tr><td>TIMIPA</td><td>—</td><td>Kokori's butler</td></tr>
<tr><td>AMANYANABO</td><td>—</td><td>Traditional ruler</td></tr>
<tr><td>SALOME</td><td>—</td><td>Market women leader</td></tr>
<tr><td>MILLICOURT</td><td>—</td><td>Abiama youth leader</td></tr>
<tr><td>DPO</td><td>—</td><td>Policeman</td></tr>
<tr><td>JOURNALIST</td><td></td><td></td></tr>
<tr><td>TELEPHONE VOICE</td><td></td><td></td></tr>
</table>

A town in Nigeria. All the actions of this play take place in the sitting room of Chief KOKORI's mansion. The time is the present.

Scene One

Lights. The sitting room in KOKORI's mansion. The room has two doors; one is opposite the audience, which leads to KOKORI's inner chamber; and the other to the left, adjacent to the audience, serves as the entrance to the house. A well furnished living room with seven-seater leather sofas – two two-seaters facing each other and a three-seater – all arranged in a semi-circle, facing the audience. Three large photographs are on the wall, depicting KOKORI's status as a family man and politician. One is a photograph of KOKORI and his wife. The other is that of two young children, a boy and a girl of about fifteen, obviously their children. Another is a photograph of KOKORI and two prominent politicians, perhaps the state Governor and the party Chairman. In the centre of the room is a round table upon which is placed a vase of artificial flowers. A large screen LED television sits on a black glass television stand, opposite the entrance. Two flags stand on the left and right side of the television – on the left side is the Nigerian flag and on the right, his party's flag. EBITI is sitting on the two-seater chair on the left. A man in his forties, he is enthusiastically flipping through the pages of a newspaper. Enter KOKORI, a man in his forties, dressed in an immaculate white etibo and a matching pair of trousers. He appears flamboyant and shows off his gold plated wristwatch intermittently, as if curious to know the time.

KOKORI: (*Excited.*) My director. (*Walking up to EBITI.*)

EBITI: (*Rising.*) Your Excellency, my Honourable, Chief, Sir, Doctor Kokori Douglas. (*They laugh loudly, shaking hands.*)

KOKORI: (*Still laughing.*) Ebiti Ebiti, the strong man of Abiama politics.

EBITI: (*Smiles.*) Who says Chief Kokori will not get a second term? The only Chairman who constructed over eight-hundred kilometre roads in less than two years. The Chairman who provided pipe-borne water and borehole pumps for all thirteen communites in Abiama.

KOKORI: (*Nods braggingly.*) Yes.

EBITI: The chair who brought the Chinese and the British to Abiama to construct an e-Library complex and the first recycling plant in the state.

KOKORI: (*Boastfully.*) It is me.

EBITI: (*Simpering.*) The first Chairman to bring the President of the Federal Republic to commission an ultra-modern market, the first of its kind in Abiama, in fact, in the whole of West Africa.

KOKORI: (*Laughing.*) That's right.

EBITI: (*Confidently.*) No man, born of a woman, can stop your victory at the polls.

KOKORI: (*Assuredly.*) No man.

EBITI: You will lead us again and again and again.

KOKORI: With your help, my able director.

EBITI: (*Smiles.*) I have done it before, haven't I? I will do it again.

KOKORI: (*Smiles.*) Absolutely! I have no doubt. Please, sit, my friend.

EBITI: Thank you. (*They sit together.*)

KOKORI: You have just returned from Abuja, haven't you?

EBITI: Only yesterday.

KOKORI: It is obvious. You look like an angel who just fell from heaven.

EBITI: (*Laughs.*) My Chief. Everytime one lands in the capital territory, you see new bridges and roads all over the place.

KOKORI: It is a result of our resources, put into good use.

EBITI: Abuja city is fabulous. The architecture and landscape, perfect. But those bridges cannot be compared to those you've built in Abiama.

KOKORI: (*Laughs.*) Chief Ebiti, sometimes I can't tell whether you flatter or speak the truth.

EBITI: No. How can I flatter my Chairman and mentor?

KOKORI: Please, don't misunderstand me, Ebiti. I am not complaining. That's the reason you are my campaign director. You will tell our people exactly what they want to hear.

EBITI: (*Laughs.*) And ignore those things they wouldn't like us to tell them.

KOKORI: (*Laughs.*) The ropes of politics.

EBITI: Certainly. We are the masters.

KOKORI: Please, make yourself at home.

EBITI: As usual.

KOKORI: (*Calling.*) Timipa! Whisky, gin or brandy?

EBITI: Something soft, please.

KOKORI: (*Surprised.*) Have you joined them, those who say it is a sin against God to drink alcohol?

EBITI: (*Laughs.*) Chief, I started drinking alcohol the day I was born.

KOKORI: That's what I thought.

EBITI: You know that Abuja is very hot. I had plenty to drink in my hotel. The air-conditioner at the Hilton Hotel cools better than a thermocool fridge. I am still recovering from all of it.

KOKORI: Soft drink then. Until you calm your nerves.

EBITI: (*Agreeing.*) Exactly.

KOKORI: (*Calling.*) Timipa!

EBITI: Has he not gone out?

> (*Enter* TIMIPA, *a young man in his twenties dressed in a pair of black trousers, white long-sleeved shirt and a blue apron, which he wears throughout the play.*)

KOKORI: Didn't you hear me call you earlier?

TIMIPA: I'm very sorry, Sir.

KOKORI: Chief Ebiti. Fanta or coke?

EBITI: Coke will be perfect. With some ice, please.

KOKORI: (*To* TIMIPA.) You heard the chief. Coke and ice … gin and lime for me.

TIMIPA: Yes, Sir. (*Exit.*)

KOKORI: How is Senator Sepribo? Certainly, you found time to see him.

EBITI: How can I touch Abuja and not see Sepribo? (*Laughs.*)

KOKORI: I wonder.

EBITI: The Senator is fine. He grows fatter by the day. You know how they chop in the hollow chamber without hassle. I think Abuja has been very kind to him. He even has the latest Land Cruiser and Jaguar. For Valentine's Day, he got his missis a Range Rover coupe and a small Honda car for school runs. He bought them in Dubai. You know he now has a holiday home there.

KOKORI: (*Surprised.*) Good for him.

EBITI: Yes. And, he supports our campaign a hundred percent.

KOKORI: Oh, good.

EBITI: He acknowledges your giant strides, too, particularly your efforts in the construction of feeder roads.

KOKORI: I am not surprised. I constructed the road from the expressway to his house.

EBITI: Indeed. He never fails to express gratitude for that gesture.

In fact, he promised a fat cheque for our campaign.

KOKORI: (*Smiles.*) That's the kind of support we need now.

EBITI: Exactly, my Chairman. I managed to meet with some of our town unions in Abuja. Most of them pledged support towards our campaign. Others promised to send cheque contributions to us through the state liaison office in Abuja. All in all, we are looking at raising another fifteen million from Abuja.

KOKORI: Remember that the Governor's German associate in Abuja also promised to donate some funds.

EBITI: I cannot forget. He will come here personally. He told me that himself.

KOKORI: Impressive work, Chief Ebiti.

EBITI: What can we do, my brother? We don't want to be left behind. Let us join other communities to move forward.

KOKORI: You are right.

(TIMIPA *enters with the tray.*)

EBITI: Timipa, your service is rather slow lately.

TIMIPA: It was the ice. Some of them had melted because I defrosted the freezer. I had to gradually select the best.

KOKORI: Don't you always have an excuse, Timipa? You would have served us first without ice.

TIMIPA: I'm sorry, Chief.

KOKORI: You are always sorry.

EBITI: I was going to say that. At least, he apologises.

TIMIPA: (*Placing the glass cups on the side tables beside* EBITI *and* KOKORI.) Here, Chief.

(*Exit.*)

KOKORI: Shouldn't he apologise?

EBITI: You are lucky, Chief. This boy is loyal and remorseful. My boy is so bold these days. He sees me in the morning and goes 'good morning', forgetting to add 'sir'. Am I his mate?

KOKORI: (*Laughs.*) You can't blame some of our domestic staff. Sometimes they feel like our lives rest in their palms.

EBITI: They really do feel that way. My cook has to taste my meals thirty minutes before I eat. I don't trust him. He may not like my face or the fact that I pay him twenty-five thousand naira every month, yet he smiles at me. Sometimes they envelop their grudges against you and when they want to take it out on you, they do so in full force.

KOKORI: They can be very very mischievous, I know.

EBITI: Imagine that Timipa spits into a sandwich he prepared for you and your family. You will never find out.

KOKORI: (*Disgustfully.*) Yuck!

EBITI: Yes. You will eat it as usual and savour it like he added extra mayonnaise.

KOKORI: The day he tries that …

EBITI: (*Cuts in.*) That day? It may never come, my Chief. If he adds saliva to your meal, you will never find out. Well, unless you catch him in the act. I know that you rarely go to the kitchen and Madam spends more time in town. We just have to pray against the bad ones. Outside that, there's really not much we can do.

KOKORI: I trust Timipa anyway. He may be slow sometimes. But that's all. (*Taking his glass up, he sips.*) Please, your coke …

EBITI: Oh, thanks. (*Takes his glass up and sips*).

KOKORI: How much have we raised outside Abiama?

EBITI: Ten million in Port Harcourt, seventeen in Lagos. Abuja promises to be good. We can expect fifteen million at the least. We've realised more than we did three years ago. So there's hope.

KOKORI: But we must put in much more effort. A lot of changes have occurred in the past three years.

EBITI: Obviously.

KOKORI: There's Facebook and Twitter now. I hear the other man has started campaigning on social media.

EBITI: Don't mind him. He is as weak as the man we beat before. It is only a poor man's strategy to campaign on social media because it's free. Real politicians pay for proper advertisement on television, radio and billboards.

KOKORI: His people likened him to Barack Obama, who used such platforms to outshine his major challenger.

EBITI: Don't mind them, Your Excellency. They don't know what they are talking about. Some of these people dwell on cheap blackmail. How can one compare America to Abiama? Those in America have computers and laptops everywhere. How many laptops can you count in Abiama? They shouldn't blackmail us with these childish tactics. I delivered Abiama to you in 2012, didn't I? Let me perform the magic again. I can assure you, we will win at least eighty-five percent of the votes this time.

KOKORI: Ebiti Ebiti.

EBITI: My name, Chief.

KOKORI: I can count on your abilities.

EBITI: I have arranged a meeting with all the journalists from the national and state television and radio. Even the private stations will be present. I've settled those in the print already to mobilise support for our campaign. You can see the way they report our rallies like no man's business. We will get to the promise land, Chief. You have no business worrying.

KOKORI: I trust you.

EBITI: They are all on your side. No one wants to be outside the winning ship.

KOKORI: We need to do more anyway. You will arrange for us to meet with the Chairman of the Council of Traditional Rulers so that I can be sure I still have their support. The market-women, too. Let us meet with their leader, Salome. I want to meet the youth leader also, he's a good mobiliser.

EBITI: Yes, I can arrange a meeting for tomorrow or the day after.

KOKORI: Let us meet them on Thursday. I'll meet with some of our Councillors tomorrow. Some of those in the opposition are contemplating running over to our party.

EBITI: They finally realise that there's no advantage in opposing the incumbent.

KOKORI: I wonder why it took this long for them to realise what is very obvious.

EBITI: We will receive them. The larger we are, the merrier.

KOKORI: Yes. If we agree to the terms between us and them, we may schedule a formal declaration ceremony for the weekend so that we can attract a larger crowd.

EBITI: We can hire some people from other local governments to swell the crowd at the campaign ground.

KOKORI: Plus, I want live media coverage of the event. It will boost our campaign and send a strong message to the opposition.

EBITI: Undoubtedly. If you can't beat them, you join them.

KOKORI: We can't run the show without His Excellency. So I must meet with the Councillors to be certain that those decamping to our party will be committed to the party at all levels of government. You will handle the package for them. I want us to arrange a little gift for the pressmen who will cover the ceremony. If you can meet me at the secretariat tomorrow, I will approve some money for this assignment.

EBITI: No problems, Chief.

KOKORI: But don't lose focus of the prize. Let us meet with the chief, the market leader and the man representing the youth.

EBITI: We will.

KOKORI: What about the Electoral Commissioner?

EBITI: I've taken care of him and his people. Don't worry about them.

KOKORI: I am moved to do more for him. I wouldn't be here today but for his determination to change the face of Abiama.

EBITI: The man is a true hero of democracy.

KOKORI: I will ensure that he receives a strong chieftaincy title when he delivers the election to our party again.

EBITI: Very perfect decision, Honourable.

KOKORI: In fact, so that he is assured of our commitments to his welfare, I will ask a driver to take one of the brand new Toyota Hiluxes the Delta Development Agency donated to us for the erosion project to him.

EBITI: My Honourable Doctor. True, I must confess that you have become more experienced than me in this business of organising campaigns. Are you sure you still need me to go on?

KOKORI: (*Laughter.*) I can't run this campaign without you, Ebiti. So rule out any idea of quitting.

EBITI: This strategy is excellent. Once we have the Electoral Commissioner on our side, who can be against us?

KOKORI: What else can we do? Politics is all about the numbers. If it's not votes, then cash can make the votes count. After all, what money cannot do, more money will do.

EBITI: (*Loud laughter.*) Certainly.

KOKORI: As a matter of fact, the Governor is very interested in what we are doing here. If we can win a second term, he'll be assured of his, too.

EBITI: Simple arithemetic.

KOKORI: As simple as ABC, yes. Let us drink to our success at the polls already.

EBITI: Oh yes, my Honourable Doctor … (*They clink glasses together.*) Cheers to your second term.

KOKORI: Ebiti Ebiti. Cheers to you, too, my brother.

(*Lights fade.*)

Scene Two

The next day. Light flickers onstage, coming on and off for about thirty seconds, then it stays on. Noises of protesters chanting 'we no go gree' outside KOKORI's residence can be heard onstage. The noise falls and increases fitfully. EBITI runs onstage from the main entrance, panting and afraid for his life. He heads straight to KOKORI's door and bangs three times with his fist. Enter KOKORI, frightened, too. Both speak in hushed tones.

KOKORI: (*Surprised.*) Ah ah, how did you get in?

EBITI: One of your boys managed to smuggle me through the gate. (*Pants terribly.*) Timipa is outside the house, he let me through this door. He may know some of those youths outside.

KOKORI: (*Looking around.*) Can you imagine those fools, good for nothing children. What are they doing this for?

EBITI: You couldn't peep to see them?

KOKORI: I did until they started throwing things at my window upstairs. I stayed out of sight.

EBITI: From their placards and chants it's obvious that they are youths from the North-East area.

KOKORI: (*Not surprised.*) Can you imagine? What is their problem? Ebiti, you must go outside now and talk to them. Ask them to go home.

EBITI: (*Surprised and anxious.*) Ah, Chief, do you want those hefty boys to send me to my untimely death? I'm not the one who should calm their nerves now. I think we should call the police.

KOKORI: (*Looks at his wristwatch.*) Are you telling me? I called the DPO over an hour ago.

EBITI: Could it be that he's afraid of them, too?

KOKORI: Look, I just want those fools out of my premises. How could I not have heard about their plans to protest?

(*Disappointed.*) You're not feeding me with information, Ebiti. You didn't know?

EBITI: How could I have heard?

KOKORI: The youth leader … the women … somebody … any one of your informants …

EBITI: Sir, these people may have taken the decision to come down here this morning. If the plan was hatched as late as 6pm yesterday, somebody would have called my attention. I am sure.

KOKORI: Please, please, please, someone must go out now to talk to them. It's getting out of hand.

(*Enter* TIMIPA *in a rush. He bends right in front of* KOKORI *and* EBITI, *who almost run into the inner chamber out of fear, and places his hands on his knees, panting seriously.*)

EBITI: (*Angry.*) Why did you run in like that? Are you mad, Timipa?

TIMIPA: I'm very sorry, Sir. Sorry.

KOKORI: (*Curiously.*) What is happening outside?

TIMIPA: (*Gasping seriously.*) Chief, those people are very angry.

EBITI: (*Angry.*) Obviously. We know that they are angry. Why?

TIMIPA: They said you have refused to finish their road and the hospital you started constructing in their community. That you stopped remitting funds to the contractor because you quarrelled with one of their sons.

KOKORI: Is that why they are making all this noise? Is it by force? Am I not the Chairman?

TIMIPA: Some of them are calling on the Economic and Financial Crimes Commission to arrest and probe you, Sir.

KOKORI: (*Surprised.*) EFCC? Can you imagine this nonsense, Ebiti? This people no longer fear the office of the Chairman. In fact, you must call the Senior Advocate to go to the highest court of the land to secure a perpetual injunction against these enemies of democracy. I am a true democrat. Ah ah, have you seen me embezzle public funds, Ebiti?

EBITI: Not at all, Sir.

KOKORI: Was it not just two months ago that I was appointed a Deacon in the Church? Don't they know that? This people have no fear at all in them.

TIMIPA: They are hitting the gate, Chief.

EBITI: Chief, this people are already going insane. Maybe you should go out there yourself and give them your assurances that you will complete the project soon. You can tell them that the contractor will report to the site tomorrow. That should calm their nerves.

KOKORI: (*Furious.*) No way, Ebiti! No way! You and I know that all funds in our coffers today are dedicated to the campaign. We cannot start now to dip our hands into those funds. We have a lot to do with money. Right now, my focus is on the campaign. I cannot be bothered about some bush people who don't know their left from right.

TIMIPA: Sir, the people out there are so many. Other passers-by have started joining them. They are very angry.

KOKORI: (*Confident.*) The police are on their way. They will deal with all of them. Don't worry. They'll be arrested very soon.

EBITI: Shouldn't you call the DPO again, Chief? Let us know when he'll get here.

KOKORI: Good idea.

(*Takes phone from his breast pocket and dials DPO. After ten seconds.*)

This man is not taking my calls. He may be conspiring with my opposition to destablise me …

(*Calls DPO again and puts phone to his ear.*) Hello, DPO …

(*The sound of the noise increases. After five seconds, the sound of various items hiting the main door can be heard sporadically. Immediately, the light starts flickering. The noise increases; KOKORI, EBITI and TIMIPA run into the inner chamber frightfully. Lights fade sharply.*)

Scene Three

Two days later. Lights. KOKORI *and* EBITI *are seated, eagerly flipping through the pages of different newspapers.*

EBITI: (*Suddenly looks at his wristwatch.*) My Honourable, it is ten o'clock already.

KOKORI: (*Looks at his wristwatch.*) Yes.

EBITI: Amanyanabo will soon be here. The others, too.

KOKORI: (*Calling.*) Timipa! He must take their names to the gate so my security people don't embarrass them, His Royal Highness especially. Those boys can be too conscious sometimes.

EBITI: Because their job is to protect you.

KOKORI: Certainly. They try too hard sometimes.

EBITI: Too hard is better, my Honourable. It is better to be safe than sorry.

KOKORI: Yes.

EBITI: Let me go to the gate myself. When your people see me they'll reduce some of the protocol.

KOKORI: I know that Amanyanabo will not come late. The man is always punctual.

EBITI: (*Rising.*) Yes. The African time is not in his dictionary. Excuse me, Sir.

KOKORI: You're excused, Director.

EBITI: (*Hastily.*) Thank you. (*Exit.*)

(*Enter* TIMIPA.)

TIMIPA: You just called, Chief.

KOKORI: (*Looks at* TIMIPA *with a mixture of suspicion and hostility.*) Just? (*Looks at his wristwatch.*) I didn't just call you, you just answered! You're beginning to drag your feet, Timipa. I called you more than five minutes ago. Are you tired of your job already?

TIMIPA: I'm very sorry, Chief.

KOKORI: You're always very sorry, Timipa. You dodged my question.

TIMIPA: (*Unsure.*) Question?

KOKORI: Are you tired of doing this job?

TIMIPA: How can I be tired of serving my master? Never! Till the day I die.

KOKORI: Well, I don't know. Lately, you have been dull in performing your duties. I don't want any form of embarrassment from you, especially when I have guests. If you feel that you need some time off, don't be afraid to ask. I'd rather have all your attention here than part of it.

TIMIPA: No, I don't want a break, Chief.

KOKORI: The food I asked that you prepare for my guests?

TIMIPA: Ready, Sir.

KOKORI: Drinks?

TIMIPA: All ready, Oga.

KOKORI: I hope you will free my ears from complaints about ice today.

TIMIPA: Well, Sir, I have a small problem at home.

KOKORI: Have I asked you to supply me with problems?

TIMIPA: Beg your pardon, Sir. My daughter …

KOKORI: (*Cuts in.*) What is the problem with your daughter, Timipa?

TIMIPA: Cough. Chest pain. I am not even sure what the problem is.

KOKORI: And you're telling me?

TIMIPA: No, Sir.

KOKORI: No?

TIMIPA: I'm very sorry, Sir.

KOKORI: Please, stop this sermon, Timipa. You apologise more than you offend me.

TIMIPA: I'm sorry …

KOKORI: (*Cuts in, splutters badly and explodes.*) No more of it, please.

TIMIPA: Thank you, Sir.

KOKORI: You haven't taken her to the hospital?

TIMIPA: I did. To the general hospital.

KOKORI: And they said?

TIMIPA: They didn't see any thing.

KOKORI: So, why are you bothered? Have you become a doctor?

TIMIPA: They asked me to go to the new teaching hospital because they have better equipment to test her lungs.

KOKORI: (*Pitying.*) So, go to the hospital.

TIMIPA: I have, Sir.

KOKORI: So?

TIMIPA: I have to buy a folder and register with four thousand naira.

KOKORI: Because the hospital is equipped with modern infrastructure and all the machines you can find in hospitals in Europe and America.

TIMIPA: Yes, Sir.

KOKORI: And you don't have the money?

TIMIPA: No, Sir.

KOKORI: I pay you thirty thousand naira every month.

TIMIPA: I used all of my last salary to settle a debt, Chief.

KOKORI: Abiama people. You like *awoof*. I know how much it cost us to build that hospital and furnish it with state-of-the-art machines. Yet, all of you want government to pay all of your bills. It is not possible, my friend. If it were a private hospital, I'm sure you'll find the money. The best things in life are not free. Look at Harvard. People who go there pay huge fees. Yet, our university people complain and go on strike every now and then because they lack basic infrastructure. You cannot have the best where people don't pay the minimum for the facilities or services they want to enjoy. I cannot take out the registration fee because of you, Timipa. Go and pay like the others and get the healthcare your daughter deserves. Here. (*Hands him a one thousand naira note.*) Add to this and take your daughter to see a doctor.

TIMIPA: (*Collects money.*) Thank you, Chief.

KOKORI: Go in already and prepare for my guests. No excuses again.

TIMIPA: Thank you, Sir.

KOKORI: I can hear their footsteps. Hurry.

TIMIPA: (*Hastily.*) Yes. (*Exit.*)

(*Enter AMANYANABO, SALOME and MILLICOURT from the entrance door. AMANYANABO is dressed in full traditional attire, depicting his status as a traditional ruler. SALOME wears a colourful blouse made from lace and ties a resembling wrapper and headgear. MILLICOURT is a young man in his early thirties. He wears a pair of jeans trousers and a t-shirt.*)

EBITI: Honourable Sir, your guests have arrived.

KOKORI: (*Happy.*) Ah, Your Royal Highness Amanyanabo.

AMANYANABO: (*Shaking* KOKORI.) Good afternoon, Your Excellency.

KOKORI: Welcome, Your Majesty. Please, sit. (AMANYANABO *sits.*) Welcome, Madam Salome. How are you today?

SALOME: (*Smiles.*) I'm fine, Honourable Kokori. It feels good to be in your mansion again.

KOKORI: Oh, thanks, Madam. Please, make yourself at home.

SALOME: Thank you. (*Sits.*)

MILLICOURT: (*Exchanging pleasantries.*) Our Honourable Chairman, Sir.

KOKORI: My youth leader.

MILLICOURT: Good afternoon, Sir.

KOKORI: Welcome. Please, sit. (*Exchanging pleasantries with* EBITI.) Thank you, Ebiti.

EBITI: Don't mention, Sir.

KOKORI: I can swear that you will do very well as my Chief of Staff and Protocol Officer when I head to the National Assembly.

EBITI: (*Loud burst of laughter.*) Anything for my Chairman.

KOKORI: Please, sit, lady and gentlemen. Let us go straight to the purpose of this meeting. (*Calling.*) Timipa!

(TIMIPA *enters.*)

TIMIPA: Chairman.

KOKORI: (*To* AMANYANABO.) Some aromatic schnapps for the Amanyanabo.

AMANYANABO: (*Smiles.*) Exactly.

KOKORI: Timipa, aromatic schnapps for Amanyanabo and myself.

TIMIPA: (*Nods.*) Yes, Sir.

KOKORI: Madam.

SALOME: Guiness extra stout.

KOKORI: And Millicourt ...

MILLICOURT: Heineken beer, please.

KOKORI: (*Smiles.*) Ebiti Ebiti.

EBITI: (*Smiles.*) My Chairman.

KOKORI: Your body should have settled now. So gin and lime.

EBITI: (*Nods.*) Gin and lime.

KOKORI: (*To* TIMIPA.) You heard them. Sharp sharp, please.

TIMIPA: At your service, Sir.

    (*Exit.*)

KOKORI: Yes. My people, I planned for this meeting to hold last week, but my campaign director was in Abuja concerning our campaign for re-election. Our message to the people is simple. We want a second term, another chance to show what our party is made of, men of timbre and calibre. Times are tough you know, the people, especially the youth, may be facing challenges of unemployment. In short, this is why some radicals stormed my gate the other day to do a silly protest. They are jobless people. Because no sane person, who is gainfully employed, will take up arms and placards to say rubbish of the government. They were obviously working for the opposition. Because our opposition's main strategy has been the use of calumny and attack. They are saying that I do not deserve a second term. I failed to do this and that. I haven't built or developed modern infrastructure. My party is corrupt. The message they have everywhere is that we have failed.

AMANYANABO: (*Shocked.*) What are you saying? The twelve traditional rulers in this LGA and I know how much our people have gained under your stewardship, and our people value your government with high esteem. You've recorded too numerous achievements in the shortest period. We are closest to this people you talk about and we feel their pulses every day. Our people think you are on the right path, Honourable.

KOKORI: (*Remembering.*) Yes. I should have asked first. I know that my guests are non-partisan, at least, in the eyes of the public. So, I should have asked to confirm that you all are still on my side.

SALOME: Ah ah! How can you say that, Chief? Where else should we go? We are always by your side, front and back. Don't mind those in the opposition. What else can they do? We know how to defeat them again, squarely!

KOKORI: So, I still have all your support? (*Looking at the faces of each of them.*)

SALOME: Why not?

MILLICOURT: Indeed, Chief.

KOKORI: Your support means more than a lot to me because of the groups you represent. Thank you. Let me allow Ebiti to brief us, so that you can return to your businesses.

EBITI: Thank you, Chief. Amanyanabo, Madam Salome, my youth leader … the major challenge before us this time around is the message that the opposition propagates about our principal and his administration. We have restricted their access to the state radio and television. But they've largely focused their campaign on fliers and social media. The crux of the message, however, has been that our chairman has failed in his first term. Thus, he doesn't deserve a second term. The question we now ask the opposition is this: if a child fails his examination as a student, shouldn't he be given a chance to repeat?

SALOME: (*Agreeing.*) That is it.

MILLICOURT: Yes.

(TIMIPA *enters with the tray.*)

KOKORI: (*Visibly angry.*) Timipa, how long does it have to take you to bring these drinks to my guests?

TIMIPA: I'm very sorry, Sir.

KOKORI: Please, drop them there and leave us immediately.

TIMIPA: Thank you, Sir. (*Serves the drinks as requested. Exit.*)

KOKORI: Please, go on, Director. I'm sorry for this boy's behaviour.

EBITI: It's okay, Chief. (*To the guests.*) What we want from you is simple. Yet, we know it's a difficult task. Chief is ready to empower you with all the resources you need so that you can mobilise your people to support his candidacy hundred percent.

AMANYANABO: Mobilising our people is not so difficult. Look at it this way. No Chairman in Abiama's history has bought brand new cars for all thirteen traditional rulers and their spouses and provided them with drivers, paid from the coffers of government. The traditional stool remains the strongest arm of government in West Africa, even though we may not be so recognised in the constitution. So, I'm certain about our support for you, Sir, our subjects, too. We are closest to them and we know that they are in this camp. Some of those youths who follow the opposition to their rallies are not from this area. They may have hired them from neigbouring communities to convince our people that they have the majority on their side. No. You shouldn't worry about our people. We will get all of their votes to you.

KOKORI: (*Grateful.*) Thank you, Amanyanabo.

SALOME: (*Smiling flagrantly.*) Chief, you know my people, you know what they need. Just provide small kola for them and the rest is history. We will mobilise support for you. All our members will be stationed across the major streets, singing your name. The opposition doesn't even stand a chance. Why?

MILLICOURT: I think Madam and His Royal Majesty have said all there is to be said. Piece of cake. We will get you all the votes you need to win a second term. Be rest assured, Chief.

KOKORI: Thank you all. I'm sure I can count on your support any day.

EBITI: (*Whispers to* KOKORI *for ten seconds.*) Yes. Like I said earlier, Honourable Kokori will empower you with enough resources to mobilise your people. Madam Salome, I will meet with you at the ultra modern market tomorrow. We will buy wrappers for all your women and we'll buy them from your shop to empower you, too.

SALOME: (*Excited.*) Ah! (*To* KOKORI.) Thank you, Chief. (*To* EBITI.) How many?

EBITI: At least five thousand pieces. We want it to get to everyone in your group.

SALOME: (*Excited.*) God will bless you, Chief Kokori.

KOKORI: (*Smiles.*) It is nothing, Madam Salome.

SALOME: (*Prayerfully.*) You will win a second term.

EBITI: (*Smiles.*) Amen.

SALOME: I will call my customer in Aba to supply all the materials you need. I hope we can go with something different from the one we used last time.

EBITI: Yes. But it should have the party's colour.

SALOME: Of course.

EBITI: We want to do more for the market-women, especially those who still rent their shops.

SALOME: (*Cuts in.*) Yes.

EBITI: We will give them an opportunity to own the shops and pay a small token to government monthly for a short period of two to three years, maybe.

SALOME: (*Excited.*) Chief, your second term is guaranteed.

EBITI: This is a new government policy. So, we cannot implement it immediately, because the election is less than a month away. But His Excellency has promised to announce this policy on the day of his swearing-in. This means that your women must do all they can to re-elect Honourable Kokori.

SALOME: (*Assuredly.*) Oh, that won't be a problem. God bless you, Sir.

EBITI: And em, our youth leader.

MILLICOURT: (*Smiling.*) Chief.

EBITI: How much money will go round your comrades?

MILLICOURT: Not easy to say now, Sir. But we can work with any amount. I will bring them together this week and share with those who attend. In fact, we are planning a one-million-man march to declare our support for His Excellency.

EBITI: (*Nods alongside* KOKORI.) Very good.

MILLICOURT: We can empower them after the march.

EBITI: Excellent. You will meet me in my office tomorrow morning so that we can discuss the details of the planned march and outline some of the things you will need to support it. I believe you will need T-shirts and face caps at least.

MILLICOURT: Obviously, Sir.

EBITI: Okay. (*Whispering to* KOKORI.)

KOKORI: Thank you, Madam Salome and Millicourt. I don't want us to take anymore of your time. You need anything, contact Chief Ebiti at my campaign office, please. Amanyanabo will wait to discuss other matters of political exigency, please.

SALOME: Okay. Thank you very much, Sir. Let me go and arrange all the materials we need.

MILLICOURT: Thank you, Chief.

(*Exit* SALOME *and* MILLICOURT.)

KOKORI: Your Highness, I said that I will speak to you myself. I respect traditional institutions and I cannot take any official decisions without imputs from you and other members of your council.

AMANYANABO: I thank you most sincerely, Honourable Kokori.

KOKORI: I will give you a token for all your members.

(*Taking out a large brown envelope from his bag*). Here. Thirty thousand dollars.

AMANYANABO (*Smiles*.) Thank you very much, Honourable.

KOKORI: That's not all, Your Majesty. I will send some more gifts to you when your council meets next week. Please, we are counting on your support especially. Once we have all of it, we can be rest assured of victory.

AMANYANABO: Yes. (*The trio all rise and shake hands. Lights fade slowly.*)

Scene Four

The evening of that day, in the same room. Lights. The stage is empty. KOKORI *and* EBITI *come onstage, laughing.*

KOKORI: We need to pull out some of those thugs from the creeks and empower them to serve as monitors for the election.

EBITI: Honourable, you know how those boys behave. Once we bring them out, they won't retreat the moment we're finished. They could make Abiama ungovernable for us later.

KOKORI: I understand your concerns. We still need very hefty men with muscles to help secure our victory.

EBITI: I agree with you, Chief.

KOKORI: Please, sit. (*They relax on the sofas.*) We will do our homework properly and everything within our powers to ensure that we don't just win, but we secure a huge majority of the votes. That boy in the opposition is too small to outsmart me.

EBITI: He's nobody. I hear he resigned from a private estate firm in town to contest this election.

KOKORI: That determined? Can you imagine?

EBITI: He must have guts though, because that's all it takes to leave a job to jump into murky waters.

KOKORI: We will defeat him anyway.

EBITI: No doubts, Your Excellency.

KOKORI: How do you see our offer to the market people and the youths? Are you confident they can deliver?

EBITI: Ah? After all that? (*Confidently.*) You're worrying too much, Oga. Victory is ours already. The only reason we are doing all these extras is to ensure that you win by a very wide margin. Besides that, I am a hundred percent certain that you will occupy Abiama House for another four years.

KOKORI: And the traditional rulers?

EBITI: (*Assertively*.) Amanyanabo will deliver. I trust him with my heart.

KOKORI: As long as you're confident.

EBITI: We should even be celebrating already.

KOKORI: We will. (*Calling*.) Timipa.

TIMIPA: (*From backstage*.) Yes, Chief. (*Enters*.)

KOKORI: (*To* EBITI.) The whole campaign has cost us a lot of money already.

TIMIPA: You called, Chief.

KOKORI: Get us something to drink.

TIMIPA: What do you want, Sir?

EBITI: (*Shocked*.) A butler doesn't know what his master likes to drink?

TIMIPA: Chief drinks according to his mood.

(KOKORI and EBITI *eagerly listen*.)

When happy, gin and lime. When sad, Seaman's Aromatic Schnapps or whisky. When the family is here, Moet & Chandon champaign, and when in the midst of very close associates, he could have Hennessy.

EBITI: What is his mood now?

TIMIPA: I can't say exactly. But he may be somewhere between Henessy, gin and lime …

EBITI: (*Laughing*.) You're not talking, Chief.

KOKORI: You have the patience for Timipa's behavioural analysis. Since he can now tell my mood, get me whatever you think I need.

TIMIPA: Hennessy?

KOKORI: Your call.

TIMIPA: (*To* EBITI.) Sir?

EBITI: I'll have whatever you bring to my friend.

TIMIPA: Thank you, Sirs. (*Exit.*)

EBITI: (*Laughing.*) He's not only loyal these days. Bold and eloquent. You should consider sending him to the university.

KOKORI: To do what, a PhD?

EBITI: No. A first degree.

KOKORI: Who says he doesn't have a degree?

EBITI: (*Shocked.*) How?

KOKORI: Timipa has a degree in Library Science.

EBITI: (*Amazed.*) Can you imagine what we've reduced our graduates to? He's a common buttler.

KOKORI: Yet, he made a second class upper in his degree.

EBITI: Our children will not see such experience in their lives.

KOKORI: Amen.

EBITI: You know, Chief, the biggest threat to any government is unemployment.

KOKORI: I know that a youth who is gainfully employed will not carry arms like those touts from the north-east area. I've asked Timipa to be patient. After all, he works for the Chairman. We will construct a community library in my second term and I will ensure that he gets a job there.

EBITI: Better. So, he'll practise what he was trained to do.

KOKORI: Certainly. These days you have graduates of Library Science and Linguistics working in banking halls. The culture is changing, yes. But I don't want to encourage such madness. A library scientist should remain in the library.

EBITI: (*Unsure.*) Yes.

KOKORI: Timipa even gets more money than those who work in the bank. Today alone, I gave him more than ten thousand naira to take his daughter to the hospital. Ask him.

EBITI: That's why he works for the Chairman.

KOKORI: (*Calling.*) Timipa.

TIMIPA: (*From backstage.*) Yes, Chief.

KOKORI: Also get us some meat.

TIMIPA: Be right there, Sir.

    (*Lights fade.*)

Scene Five

One week to election Saturday. Lights come on in KOKORI's living room. The stage is empty and quiet for a minute. Enter EBITI, SALOME and MILLICOURT, appearing very tired. They all go to sit.

EBITI: (*Calling.*) Timipa.

SALOME: (*Looking around.*) Oga Ebiti, it doesn't appear Timipa is at home.

MILLICOURT: I don't think he is. The house is too quiet to have anyone around.

EBITI: But you heard the protocol man at the gate say that he didn't go out.

MILLICOURT: You know this people at the gate, they may have fallen asleep when the guy stepped out. How many security personnel actually stay up at nights or in the day to guard their masters? In fact, most of them sleep deeper than their ogas. So you can't take their word for it.

EBITI: (*Suddenly remembers.*) Come to think of it, security is one of our biggest challenges in Abiama, and Chairman doesn't seem to possess the political will to tackle it. One must be blunt. In all his almost four years, nothing has been done in that area.

MILLICOURT: You know, I thought I was alone. My thoughts exactly. One even wonders what happened to the local vigilante groups. They were very good in the past.

EBITI: You see, I know Chief very well. I met him in our heydays at the university. He lives in a world of his imagination. When we came on board, I warned him not to jettison the vigilante groups, but he insisted. The man does not give a hoot about the common man. He grew up with a silver spoon in his mouth. His parents paid his fees up to master's level and even assured to send him abroad for doctoral studies. He should have gone, but he was caught up in local politics.

SALOME: (*Shocked.*) I thought you people call him doctor?

EBITI: Thanks to the private university on the main express. They awarded him with an honorary doctorate degree because he used taxpayers' money to tar the road to the university.

MILLICOURT: (*Surprised.*) So it's honorary?

EBITI: Yes.

SALOME: Chief likes titles. (*Mimicking.*) Honourable, Chief, Doctor, Sir … for just one person.

EBITI: That's how we live in this part of the world.

SALOME: What really happened to him?

EBITI: (*Curious.*) How do you mean?

SALOME: He started very well. He made outstanding promises when he campaigned and had one of the best manifestos ever delivered in the state. Yes, his first hundred days in office were great, but he lost it along the way. Unfortunately we cannot say this to his face, since we also benefit from his largesse. But I must be frank, Chief Ebiti, my women are skeptical about Chief. He made too many promises last time that he failed to keep. How then can we be hopeful for his new promises? He may end up even badly, knowing that this is his final term.

EBITI: This is why I've never thought it a wise idea to give people a second term in politics. They run out of ideas in their first term and their second term particularly focuses on dishing out personal vendettas.

MILLICOURT: You're Chief's re-election coordinator. Yet, you think the second term is inconsequential?

EBITI: My dear Millicourt, you will not understand some of the decisions we have to live with in politics. I may not agree with the man, but he pays my bills. He also pays me to believe in him. I may be pretending if you choose to see it that way, but I'm paid to do the job.

SALOME: Chief is not a bad man. But, call a spade a spade. He and some of his people at the top share Abiama cake amongst themselves and forget to throw the crumbs to those below them. You noticed how he and the Councillors change their official cars every year. He bought cars for all traditional rulers and the VIPs in Abiama. Our monthly allocations hiked recently. Yet, Chief has refused to recommence issuing bursaries to university students from Abiama. The man before him disbursed bursaries to tertiary students for all four years he served as our Chairman.

EBITI: (*Sad face.*) It's a pity really. I know that Oga doesn't care so much about the poor. His government is of the rich, for the rich and by the rich.

SALOME: We must overcome this madness somehow. Our people are dying. Look at the hospital he built for the rich alone. He couldn't add to the classroom blocks in the secondary schools. Yet, he is building his private school in Abiama. I am sure, with taxpayers' money.

EBITI: He believes he's the best thing to have happened to Abiama and you cannot tell him otherwise.

(*A phone in* MILLICOURT's *breast pocket rings.*)

MILLICOURT: Hello … Right now? I am at the chief's residence. Let us resolve this later, please … Thank you.

(*After five seconds.*)

It was my deputy. This people are complaining seriously about Chief. They do not think that he's the best candidate for this election and I'm finding it so difficult to convince them.

EBITI: (*Not surprised.*) What are they saying?

MILLICOURT: Oga, isn't it obvious that we've not made any significant progress in Abiama since your man became our Chairman?

EBITI: They want to vote the opposition?

MILLICOURT: (*Contemplates.*) Maybe.

EBITI: Is the devil you know not better than the one you don't know?

SALOME: (*Cuts in.*) Director, Sir, this matter has gone beyond the devil you know and the one you don't.

EBITI: Those who live in glass houses don't owe us more than daily wages if we work for them. Let's take it easy. Those who go to seek revenge may end up being the ones who are burned.

MILLICOURT: What are you saying?

EBITI: Any attempt to make the Honourable fail in his re-election bid may have a bad omen. We might end up hurting ourselves. In the end, we may find ourselves displaced.

MILLICOURT: Sir, is it not better that we get a good Chairman who will be committed to doing good things in Abiama, even if we are not favoured by his administration? Chief is not poor, just wicked enough to grab all the funds allocated to Abiama and yet, he gives those of us who support him peanuts. Don't you realise he now has one of the biggest houses in Port Harcourt GRA?

EBITI: It didn't cost him so much to buy that house. In fact, he got it through the state government's privatisation scheme. The house was used as a guest house for the Deputy Governor in the 1970s.

MILLICOURT: What does the matter anyway? I am sure Chief has hidden all manner of currencies under the ground. For all you know, they may be buried right beneath us.

SALOME: (*Laughs.*) My brother, Millicourt, politicians are the same everywhere. It's just like marriage. A man quarrels with his wife because she nags and he goes out to meet his mistress because she doesn't. The moment he marries the mistress, he discovers that she even nags more than the former. They are the same.

EBITI: Yet, you don't agree with me that the devil you know is a better devil?

SALOME: Our Honourable is not even the devil you know. If not that he empowers me by patronising my business, what else do I know about him? Can I say that I know him?

(KOKORI *enters suddenly.* EBITI, SALOME *and* MILLICOURT *rise immediately.*)

EBITI: Your Excellency, my Honourable, Chief, Sir, Doctor Kokori.

KOKORI: (*Laughing.*) Ebiti Ebiti. (*Shake hands.*) My director. Madam Salome, Millicourt.

SALOME/MILLICOURT: (*Simultaneously.*) Welcome, Sir.

KOKORI: I hope I didn't keep you waiting for too long. Make yourselves at home. Please, sit. Has Timipa offered you anything? Food, water?

EBITI: No, not a glimpse of him. Is he at home? He may have gone to the market.

KOKORI: (*Certain.*) No. He doesn't go to the market twice in one week. (*Calling.*) Timipa.

(*Enter* TIMIPA.)

TIMIPA: (*To* KOKORI.) Good afternoon, Sir. (*To the others.*) Good afternoon.

KOKORI: Good afternoon. You didn't offer them something to eat or drink.

TIMIPA: I thought you just came in, Sir.

KOKORI: Yes. But they were here before me.

TIMIPA: I didn't hear them come in, Sir.

KOKORI: Ebiti, what time did you get here?

EBITI: (*Looks at his wristwatch.*) At about noon.

KOKORI: (*To* TIMIPA.) And you had no idea that three adults came into your house? Are you not joking?

TIMIPA: They may have come in quietly. I'm sorry, Chief.

KOKORI: Get us something to drink, while you prepare lunch for four.

SALOME: Honourable, I may not stay for lunch. Some of my people are waiting to see me at the shop.

KOKORI: Okay. You heard Madam, Timipa.

TIMIPA: Yes, Chief. Lunch will be served for three.

SALOME: Thank you, Sir.

KOKORI: Maybe get us water to drink first.

TIMIPA: Thank you, Chief. (*Exit.*)

EBITI: He thanks you for everything.

KOKORI: Don't mind him. (*Rubbing his palms together.*) So, my people, what's the latest?

EBITI: We were just analysing some of our activities before you came in. Everything has been going well as planned. Right now, it all boils down to funds. Everyone, women, men and the youths, have been mobilised for the D-Day.

KOKORI: Okay, Millicourt.

MILLICOURT: Honourable.

KOKORI: Some of your youths tried to stone my convoy with eggs this morning.

MILLICOURT: (*Cutting in, surprised.*) No. They couldn't have been Abiama youths, maybe hooligans from neigbouring communities.

EBITI: (*Surprised.*) Ah ah.

KOKORI: If it were not for the bravery of my driver, the incident might have resulted in a bad accident. They are perhaps the same people who demonstrated in front of my house two weeks ago. And the election is here already. I don't want touts like them to ruin our chances and defeat all we've worked for.

MILLICOURT: No, Sir. Perhaps, they've woken up to the realisation that they have no chances at victory in the upcoming poll. The opposition.

EBITI: That is true, Chief.

KOKORI: I hope it is. (*To* SALOME.) Madam, I hope we are not keeping you away from your people.

SALOME: (*Looking at her wristwatch.*) No problems, Sir.

KOKORI: It's okay to leave now if you want to meet up with your appointment. We will see you tomorrow, before the debate.

SALOME: Okay Chief. I will leave then. (*Rising.*)

KOKORI: Thank you, Madam.

SALOME: Thank you, Sir.

KOKORI: (*Looks at his wristwatch.*) Timipa hasn't come out with the water? (*Angry, calling*) Timipa. Please, wait a minute, Madam.

SALOME: Alright, Sir.

(*Enter* TIMIPA *with a tray and four bottles of mineral water.*)

KOKORI: What is happening to you, Timipa?

TIMIPA: I'm very sorry, Sir.

KOKORI: (*Angry.*) I asked for an answer not an apology. What is happening?

TIMIPA: Nothing, Sir.

KOKORI: Nothing?

TIMIPA: Yes, Sir.

KOKORI: Drop that tray and get out of this place.

TIMIPA: I'm sorry, Sir. (*Drops tray on centre table.*) I'm sorry, Sir.

KOKORI: Leave my sight.

TIMIPA: Sorry. (*Exit.*)

KOKORI: (*To* SALOME.) Madam, please, take a bottle of water.

SALOME: Thank you, Sir. (*Picks a bottle of water.*) I must leave now, Sir.

KOKORI: Okay, Madam. Cheers.

SALOME: Bye, Sir. Oga Ebiti, see you tomorrow.

EBITI: Okay, Madam.

(*Exit* SALOME.)

KOKORI: Ebiti, you must have gotten some of the questions for our debate tomorrow.

EBITI: Quite the contrary, Chief. You see, the consortium of journalists that came together for this debate are different from those who are in our camp.

KOKORI: So what? Get them to join us.

EBITI: Not so easy, Honourable.

KOKORI: Come, come, Ebiti, I am relying on you for the best. Surely, every man or woman has got a price. What's theirs? You should find out. I cannot appear with my opponent in the public and not know what jibes they plan to throw my way. For all we know, there could be a connivance between them, the opposition and this consortium you talk about.

EBITI: No. You are wrong entirely. These journalists were hired specifically for the debate by an international NGO, partnering with another NGO, locally based in Abiama.

KOKORI: You don't know who runs this local NGO?

EBITI: I will find out, Chief.

KOKORI: Well, you must do so immediately. We do not have all the time now to gamble. We must do all that is within our power to ensure that everything works in our favour.

EBITI: You are right, Sir. I'll wrap this up today, no matter what.

KOKORI: Please.

EBITI: No problem. (*Phone rings in his breast pocket, takes the phone out and looks at it.*) Excuse me, Chief. I have to take this call.

KOKORI: Okay, Ebiti.

EBITI: Be right back. (*Exit.*)

KOKORI: Millicourt, you are very quiet.

MILLICOURT: No, Sir.

KOKORI: Please, have some water.

MILLICOURT: Thank you, Sir. (*Takes a bottle of water from the tray.*) I must leave now too. But I'll be present at the debate tomorrow.

KOKORI: You must come with your people to cheer me up.

MILLICOURT: Certainly, we'll endeavour to be present. (*Rising.*) Thank you, Chief.

KOKORI: See you.

> (*Exit* MILLICOURT. *After a minute,* KOKORI *makes an exit to his chamber. He re-enters with some sheets of paper, then goes back to sit. He starts practising for his speech by reading from the sheets.*)

KOKORI: Fellow Abiamans, I am delighted and proud whenever I get the opportunity to inform you of our achievements and the determination of my administration to continue to drive more development in our communities. As a government, we want to ensure good governance by sustaining a government of discipline, leadership by example and obviously, people-centred policies. In the past three plus years, the priority of our party has been to protect the life of all Abiamans and to make you safe in your homes, on the streets, and to enable you move from one point to another at any hour of the day or night without the fear for your safety or life. We know that sustaining a safe and secure Abiama cannot be possible with poverty and unemployment. For this, we believe that you will continue to give us your mandate as we hope to create full and gainful jobs for all those willing and able to work. We will re-focus our attention on the agriculture sector to ensure that over ten thousand new jobs are created within six months of our second inauguration. We will provide critical infrastructure and social services in all thirteen communities and rapidly increase the output of food crops to reduce hunger and starvation amongst our people. In education, we believe that this is a right for all human beings. Therefore, every Abiama citizen is entitled to quality education. We will ensure that all Abiamans are literate and able to communicate in major world languages, including our mother tongue. We will train Abiamans at various levels of manpower to transform the nation as a whole.

(*Enter* EBITI.)

EBITI: Chief.

KOKORI: Ebiti, I thought you had gone.

EBITI: No. I was on the phone, outside. I tried to reach this people on the phone.

KOKORI: (*Curious.*) Who?

EBITI: The media consortium. In fact, the local organiser is refusing to expose the questions for tomorrow's debate.

KOKORI: Why? Is he not from Abiama?

EBITI: She is. She insists that it is not the norm.

KOKORI: But I am the incumbent and this should be part of the entitlements I enjoy.

EBITI: She's strong-headed, Chief.

KOKORI: She must have a price. Find out.

EBITI: I'm not sure about that, Chief.

KOKORI: Let me speak to her directly. Call her now.

EBITI: She's refusing to speak to candidates directly.

KOKORI: (*Amazed.*) You didn't speak to her?

EBITI: I spoke to her research assistant.

KOKORI: (*Amazed.*) She has a research assistant?

EBITI: Yes. Another young lady with an accent.

KOKORI: An accent?

EBITI: Yes. British, I think.

KOKORI: Oh. They have a price. Everyone does!

EBITI: I understand that both of them are doctoral students of Journalism in the United Kingdom and this is part of their research.

KOKORI: Then, they cannot come to Abiama and ask the incumbent questions from a black box. Ebiti, I will not take part in a debate without seeing the questions beforehand. Find out what they want. I will give them twofold. What if I am asked a question I cannot answer? On live television? I cannot be embarrassed by anyone just like that. Let alone, two small journalists from the UK. At least, I should enjoy the privileges that come with being the incumbent.

EBITI: I will call them again. There must be something we can arrange.

KOKORI: Sure, they have a price. Find out what it is.

EBITI: Let me go out and call her.

KOKORI: No, Ebiti. Call her here now, before me. (*Drops sheets of paper on side stool.*)

EBITI: (*Reluctantly.*) Okay. (*Dials a number on his phone and puts the phone to his ear.*)

KOKORI: Speakerphone.

EBITI: (*Puts the call on speakerphone reluctantly.*) Hello, Madam.

TELEPHONE VOICE: (*With strong British accent.*) Good afternoon. How can I help?

EBITI: I am calling on behalf of His Excellency, the Honourable, Chief, Sir, Doctor Kokori Douglas, *mfr, mni, fnim,* the Chairman of Abiama LG.

TELEPHONE VOICE: (*Firmly.*) Yes, how can I help?

EBITI: I have called regarding your debate tomorrow.

TELEPHONE VOICE: You mean the debate between the council chairman contenders?

EBITI: Yes.

TELEPHONE VOICE: Then it's not my debate. We are only coordinators. The debate is between your candidate and Mr Warigbani.

EBITI: Indeed.

TELEPHONE VOICE: So, what can I do for you?

EBITI: We like to speak with our daughter directly …

TELEPHONE VOICE: (*Cutting in.*) Sir, I think you called earlier, less than thirty minutes ago. And like I told you then, she's very busy. I am her research assistant. Whatever you want to say to her, you can say to me. I will pass it on to her immediately she's free.

EBITI: My Chairman wants to see the draft of questions your team plans to ask him.

TELEPHONE VOICE: Sir, I believe I made myself very clear when we spoke earlier. It is not the norm to present questions for a debate to the debaters before the debate. That's why it is what it is.

EBITI: But we are the incumbent.

TELEPHONE VOICE: Makes no difference. If the intention of the debate is to learn about the policies you want to present to your electorate, such policies should be stuck in your head. By the way, you're allowed to come in with your manifestos and as many documents and books as you wish to use.

EBITI: Yes. We still insist on seeing those questions.

TELEPHONE VOICE: (*Cutting in.*) Excuse me, Sir. There's nothing we can do about your request, I'm afraid.

KOKORI: Young lady, this is Honourable Kokori speaking.

TELEPHONE VOICE: Good afternoon, Sir.

KOKORI: Why are you making a big deal out of the questions for tomorrow's debate? You're sure you have not been bought by my opposition?

TELEPHONE VOICE: (*Cutting in.*) I beg your pardon, Sir! I am not quite clear about your statement.

KOKORI: You are refusing to show us the questions you intend to ask tomorrow.

TELEPHONE VOICE: Yes, Sir. We can't do that.

KOKORI: (*Braggingly.*) I am the incumbent.

TELEPHONE VOICE: The more reason. Some of these questions haven't come in. So, I wonder why we are so disturbed about them, Sir.

KOKORI: (*Curious.*) Where are the questions coming from?

TELEPHONE VOICE: We expect our online audience to ask questions via Facebook, Twitter and other platforms.

KOKORI: Facebook?

TELEPHONE VOICE: And other platforms, yes.

KOKORI: I know that we all have a price. What do you want to make these questions available to us?

TELEPHONE VOICE: I beg your pardon, Sir. We are not for sale.

KOKORI: Two million?

TELEPHONE VOICE: (*Shocked.*) Excuse me.

KOKORI: Five?

TELEPHONE VOICE: I'm done having this conversation, Sir. We will see you on the podium tomorrow. Goodbye. (*Phone goes off.*)

KOKORI: Can you imagine? This girl has no respect for age. Is she not a child?

EBITI: I believe she is.

KOKORI: Find out who she is and what she wants. She must have a price. Everyone has.

EBITI: Okay, Chief.

KOKORI: Please. (*Looks at his wristwatch.*) The debate comes up in a little over twenty hours.

EBITI: (*Looks at his wristwatch.*) Yes, Chief.

KOKORI: I will not make an appearance at the debate if those children fail to show me the questions they want to ask. She talked about Facebook. Is that not the same platform Warigbani is using to campaign against me?

EBITI: It is.

KOKORI: And you called it the platform for the weak? They want to hurt our chances intentionally and I won't give them that opportunity. Find out what they want. I will pay them twofold.

EBITI: Let me do that right away, Chief.

KOKORI: Please, Ebiti. I am counting on you to get us out of this. No questions, no debate.

EBITI: Okay, Sir. I will inform you of the outcome.

KOKORI: Thank you, Ebiti. As soon as you contact them, please, let me know.

EBITI: (*Rising.*) Okay, Chief. (*Exit.*)

KOKORI: British or no British, everyone has a price. (*Takes up the sheets of paper from the side stool.*)

(*Enter* TIMIPA.)

TIMIPA: Lunch is served, Chief.

KOKORI: Thank you, Timipa. I will be eating alone this afternoon. Ebiti may return soon, anyway.

TIMIPA: Yes, Chief. (*Still standing.*) Sir, you know that I live in the village …

KOKORI: (*Cuts in.*) Another problem … What is it, Timipa?

TIMIPA: Your people are not happy, Chief.

KOKORI: (*Casually.*) Ebiti doesn't say that.

TIMIPA: He doesn't tell you everything.

KOKORI: And you do?

TIMIPA: Chief Ebiti lives in GRA. He doesn't see the sufferings of our people, what they go through day by day.

KOKORI: Ebiti is my eyes, Timipa. If what you say is true, he should have told me long ago.

TIMIPA: He won't. He benefits from your administration, Sir.

KOKORI: And you don't?

TIMIPA: Not as much as he.

KOKORI: Any other thing?

TIMIPA: (*Contemplatively.*) Sir, you should be wary of your friends. You musn't trust them always. They may just be wolves in sheep's clothing.

KOKORI: (*Interested.*) What are you saying, Timipa?

TIMIPA: Your friends, Sir.

KOKORI: Which one of my friends do you talk about?

TIMIPA: All of them.

KOKORI: Why … What the devil's the matter with you?

TIMIPA: I will not trust them, Sir. Just now they were all gratitude and duty. Before you came in, different. They can't be on your side, Chief.

KOKORI: O shut up, Timipa. What do you know?

TIMIPA: What, would you have me tell a lie?

KOKORI: But, for heaven's sake! What are you saying? You say I should be careful. You say I shouldn't trust my friends. What should I be careful about? Who should I not trust?

TIMIPA: Then, Sir, I must tell you plainly, that Chief Ebiti …

KOKORI: (*Cuts in.*) Timipa, did you touch my bottle of whisky? (*Convinced.*) Sure enough, it must have been so. You had some whisky and now you're going off key. Please, have my lunch ready on the table. Then, off to your quarters. I will call when I need you.

TIMIPA: I'm sorry, Sir.

KOKORI: Don't give me those apologies now. I'm not looking for it. Go.

TIMIPA: Thank you. (*Exit.*)

(*Lights fade.*)

Scene Six

Lights. The morning after the debate. KOKORI's sitting room appears scattered, the room was mugged at night. TIMIPA is seen on stage trying to put the room in order. Enter KOKORI.

KOKORI: (*Surprised.*) Timipa, what happened here?

TIMIPA: I came in five minutes ago, Chief.

KOKORI: And?

TIMIPA: I met the room in this mess.

KOKORI: (*Amazed.*) Someone broke into my official residence?

TIMIPA: It appears so, Sir. The keyhole was tampered with. I informed the security men at the gate. None of them noticed any signs of intrusion. They …

KOKORI: (*Cuts in.*) Don't touch a thing. Let me call the District Police Officer immediately.

(*Dials DPO and places the phone on his ear. After five seconds.*)

Ah, DPO … Yes, good morning.

(*Surprised.*)

You're aware my house was robbed? Gracious me. You're on your way already … Very good. Thank you.

(*Call ends.*)

This has never happened before. Strangers now come to Abiama to steal? We must get to the root of the matter.

(*Calls* EBITI *on his phone.*)

Chief Ebiti, can you imagine that my house was robbed? Call my personal secretary and … In fact, I want us to call a meeting this morning. I've called the DPO already. You must come also. We must constitute a committee this morning that will investigate this incident. How is it possible? If a stranger could break all security protocol and break into the residence of the Chairman, this means that my people can no longer be safe in their homes.

(*After five seconds, surprised.*)

Ah, you're on your way already … You're with the police chief … You should have said that long ago. Okay. I will wait for you two to get here. Bye.

(*Hangs up.*)

What is happening?

(*Sits.*)

Go inside, Timipa.

TIMIPA: Okay, Sir. (*There's a knock on the door.*)

KOKORI: Check who's at the door.

TIMIPA: Okay, Sir. (*Walks up to the door. Opens it. Then enter EBITI and DPO, a young man dressed in black and blue police uniform.*)

KOKORI: (*Rising.*) Eh heh, Chief Ebiti, DPO. I can't understand, DPO. What is happening? How can somebody break my security protocol and come into my house? I know that the thief came in from outside Abiama to do this.

DPO: Good morning, Chief. We have apprehended the intruder.

KOKORI: (*Amazed.*) Ah ah, how did you catch him? Where did he come from?

DPO: Abiama.

KOKORI: (*Doubtfully.*) No. He couldn't have come from Abiama. You should interrogate him properly.

DPO: We have done that already, Chief. In fact, he reported to the station himself and confessed this morning.

KOKORI: Unless, the opposition hired him to assassinate me. They must be aware already that I'm leading in the polls.

DPO: Contrary to that, Chief. If his mission was to assassinate you, he should have tampered with the door leading to your inner chambers. I'm sure he didn't.

KOKORI: So?

DPO: Did you notice anything that he might have taken away from here?

KOKORI: No, Officer, not yet. Beat this man up, let him start telling who sent him to my house. That's what I am concerned about, not any missing items.

DPO: We don't have to beat him up, Sir. The young man told us that he broke into your house because he was starved of food for days and was hungry. Yet, he learnt that food was in abundance here.

KOKORI: (*Amazed.*) What? You are joking. How can you tell me that he did this just for food?

DPO: (*Pointing at a dirty plate on the floor.*) That must have been the plate he used to eat.

KOKORI: (*Sharply.*) That was my dinner. I left it on the table. I didn't touch the food.

DPO: And that, perhaps, was what stopped him from breaking through your inner chamber. If he hadn't seen the food on the table, he may have gone in search of food inside.

KOKORI: (*With horror.*) What?

DPO: Yes.

KOKORI: And you say he is from Abiama?

DPO: Indeed.

KOKORI: (*Pointedly.*) I am not convinced that he broke into this house for a plate of food. Why didn't he go elsewhere? There are many restuarants in Abiama. Why come here? Ebiti.

EBITI: (*Absentmindedly.*) What did you say, Chief?

KOKORI: The thief. Can you believe that he just broke into my house for a plate of meal?

EBITI: (*Coughs.*) Many things happen these days, Chief. A lot is possible. He may be telling the truth, who knows? (*Clears his throat.*) I think that this is an unnecessary distraction. We can ignore this episode and deal with it after the election, else we'll give the opposition something to talk about.

KOKORI: DPO.

DPO: Yes, Chief.

KOKORI: Let the man remain in your custody. Also, do not suspend your interrogation or any investigation surrounding this intruder. He may have more confessions to make. I was already preparing to constitute a high powered committee to carry out a proper and well coordinated investigation. I do not want this to happen again. Let this not get to the public. We will deal with the man next week.

DPO: Okay, Chief. I must head back to the station now. In the meantime, you may just look around to see if any valuable item is missing from the room. If any, feel free to inform me, Sir.

KOKORI: Thank you, Officer.

(*Exit* DPO.)

EBITI: Chief, we must do everything within our powers to keep this incident away from the press.

KOKORI: (*With rage.*) Timipa! I will hold you responsible for this break-in. You have connived with my enemies to disgrace me.

TIMIPA: (*Shocked.*) How can I do that, Sir? I took an oath and swore allegiance to you and your office.

KOKORI: (*Cuts in.*) What does it matter? Allegiance, oath ... What does it all mean any more?

EBITI: Please, calm down, Chief.

TIMIPA: I will never do anything to cause harm to you or your family, Chief. I swear on the grave of my grandfather.

KOKORI: (*Sighs.*) Leave my sight immediately. (*Sternly.*) Nobody must say anything about this to the press or anyone outside this house. (*Fiercely.*) Am I clear, Timipa?

TIMIPA: Yes, Sir.

KOKORI: Leave.

TIMIPA: I'm sorry, Sir. (*Exit.*)

KOKORI: Chief Ebiti, you don't tell me that my people are hungry.

EBITI: They are not hungry, Honourable.

KOKORI: (*Looking around.*) And the man who did all this?

EBITI: Chief, you know that no matter how hard you work, you cannot touch the lives of every living person positively. For the majority, at least, you have made a significant difference in their lives.

KOKORI: If a man will go this far for a plate of food, then my people cannot be happy.

EBITI: This incident should not worry you, Chief. It is a distraction. (*Changing the subject.*) Yesterday's debate went ahead without you.

KOKORI: (*Shocked, slightly impatient.*) How?

EBITI: The organisers turned the debate into an avenue for Mr Warigbani to speak his manifesto and vision to the people. Afterwards, they had a question and answer session.

KOKORI: (*Goes to sit.*) I told you that those people are working with the opposition. (*Worried.*) Collaborators, the handwriting on the wall was so obvious. I smelt mischief on their part. Anyway, what was the reaction from the audience?

EBITI: The criticisms against the opposition's planned demolition of some of the slums came out hard.

KOKORI: Good. Please, sit.

EBITI: (*Sitting.*) In fact, most questions focused on it after the issue was raised by a student in the audience.

KOKORI: Very good. And my absence?

EBITI: Not much centred on it. However, I think that the opposition planted people in the audience to bring it up.

KOKORI: And they succeeded?

EBITI: Things didn't work exactly in their favour. Shouldn't you have watched it, Sir? It was on live TV.

KOKORI: I was too tired and drunk.

EBITI: Oh!

KOKORI: Many things on my mind.

EBITI: I can understand, Chief.

KOKORI: You must do everything possible to keep this break-in incident away from the press and the public.

EBITI: (*Assuredly.*) Not a problem, Sir.

KOKORI: Have we concluded arrangements with the hotel?

EBITI: Accomodation for the observer team?

KOKORI: Yes.

EBITI: Yes. We've deposited eighty percent of the bill. Thirty-two rooms in total.

KOKORI: We will cover their meals, too, and transport.

EBITI: I know, Sir.

KOKORI: The boys from the press?

EBITI: We will pay honorarium to the local press and take care of their transport and feeding. But we must do this and provide accommodation for the press boys coming in from town.

KOKORI: Ok. How's your account?

EBITI: Well, em …

KOKORI: (*Cuts in.*) The exact status. I don't want us making any mistakes. You must begin now to tie loose ends. All.

EBITI: Certainly.

KOKORI: I will give you some money, two million in cash and another seven in cheque.

EBITI: (*Smiles.*) Okay, Sir.

KOKORI: That should take care of further logistics.

EBITI: (*With concern.*) Top priority, Chief. I hope you've managed to keep in touch with the Electoral Commissioner.

KOKORI: Yes. I've called him consistently on a daily basis to make certain that he is still on our side. I will speak to him later this evening.

EBITI: He has the final say. Not the voters.

KOKORI: Indeed. He is the umpire of this game. He decides who wins.

EBITI: I have arranged for an interview with one of the local papers so that you can appear on the Thursday edition. It will be a full centrepage piece. We are hoping that this will pull the undecided voters to our side.

KOKORI: Very good, Ebiti.

EBITI: The journalist may come to your office at noon today.

KOKORI: (*Cuts in.*) No. Let him meet me here at home. Too many people have besieged my office these days to beg for one favour or another. They feel that I'll be obliged to grant their requests because I need their votes now. I'll spend the coming days here and work from home. So let him meet me here.

EBITI: This journalist is a woman.

KOKORI: Better.

EBITI: She's the political correspondent of *Abiama Herald*. I will call her later to confirm the time.

KOKORI: (*With interest.*) Why not call her now? The D-day is barely a week.

EBITI: (*Indifferently.*) Okay, Chief. (*Takes his phone, dials the number and puts the phone to his ear.*) Hello, Reporter, when did you say that you want to speak to Honourable? Oh now … You are on your way already?

KOKORI: (*Cuts in.*) Even better.

EBITI: Good. The chief is ready for you. But you will not meet me here. Eh heh. Thank you. (*Hangs up.*)

KOKORI: You are leaving already?

EBITI: To take care of other loose ends, yes.

KOKORI: The journalist will be here soon, I suspect.

EBITI: Yes, Chief.

KOKORI: (*Calls quietly.*) Timipa. (*Louder.*) Timipa.

TIMIPA: (*From inside one of the rooms.*) Yes, Chief.(*Enter.*)

KOKORI: Clear this place up immediately. I'm expecting someone.

TIMIPA: Okay, Sir. (*Starts putting the room in order.*)

KOKORI: (*Rising.*) I will go inside to change. I believe the journalist may want to take some photographs, too.

EBITI: I suppose. (*Rising.*)

KOKORI: Give her name to the protocol people at the gate so they don't embarrass her.

EBITI: Okay, Chief. I will return in the afternoon.

KOKORI: Please, do.

EBITI: I will. (*Exit.*)

KOKORI: Do that quickly, Timipa.

TIMIPA: Yes, Chief.

> (*Exit* KOKORI. *After thirty seconds,* TIMIPA *leaves the stage. The stage is quiet for a minute. Then, a knock is heard on the door for about ten seconds. Enter* TIMIPA, *who walks straight to the door.*)

TIMIPA: (*Shouts.*) Who? (*No reply. He opens the door.*) Are you the guest Honourable is expecting?

JOURNALIST: (*Entering.*) Yes. I'm here for a scheduled interview. I'm a reporter with *Abiama Herald*.

TIMIPA: Oh. Let me get the chief. Please, sit.

JOURNALIST: (*Grateful.*) Thank you.

TIMIPA: He would usually ask that you make yourself at home. So I beg you to.

JOURNALIST: (*Smiles.*) Thank you.

TIMIPA: I will let him know that you're here.

JOURNALIST: (*Looking around.*) Many thanks.

> (*Exit* TIMIPA.)

KOKORI: (*Entering.*) My young lady.

JOURNALIST: (*Rises on seeing* KOKORI, *chuckles.*) Good morning, Honourable Kokori.

KOKORI: Good morning, beautiful lady. (*They shake hands.*) You must be the most beautiful journalist in Abiama.

JOURNALIST: (*Enticingly.*) I feel flattered, Chief.

KOKORI: Please, sit. (*They sit together.*) Make yourself at home.

JOURNALIST: (*Smiles.*) Your butler told me you'll say that.

KOKORI: Yes. He knows me well enough. What do you want to eat, drink?

JOURNALIST: Nothing, Sir. I don't eat or drink this early.

KOKORI: You're watching your weight?

JOURNALIST: (*Laughing.*) No, Sir. I have my first meal at eleven, just before noon.

KOKORI: Then, that must be the secret of your good looks.

JOURNALIST: (*Smiles.*) You flatter too much, Chief.

KOKORI: Flatter? Even when I speak the truth? (*They both laugh.*) You're here to do an interview.

JOURNALIST: Yes.

KOKORI: I'm allowed to have a drink while you ask your questions?

JOURNALIST: Why not, Sir?

KOKORI: (*Calling.*) Timipa.

TIMIPA: (*Entering.*) Yes, Chief.

KOKORI: A glass of whisky for me.

TIMIPA: Nothing for the young lady?

KOKORI: Nothing.

TIMIPA: Right away, Sir. (*Exit.*)

KOKORI: Yes. Your questions …

JOURNALIST: (*Cuts in.*) Don't worry, Chief. I'm not here to ask questions that won't help you win Saturday's election. We want to do a good profile interview that will portray you as the people's candidate.

KOKORI: (*Happy.*) Lovely.

(*Enter* TIMIPA *with the tray.*)

TIMIPA: Your whisky, Sir.

KOKORI: (*Directing* TIMIPA *to the side stool.*) Here, drop it.

TIMIPA: (*Places the glass on the stool.*) Thank you, Chief. (*Exit.*)

KOKORI: (*Gulps down his drink.*) Yes. Let's get the ball rolling.

JOURNALIST: (*Putting on her audio recorder, hanging on her neck.*) Ready?

KOKORI: I'm all yours. (*Curious.*) Wait a minute, shouldn't that recorder be hanging on my neck?

JOURNALIST: (*Laughs.*) No, Chief. It is powerful enough to take all that is said in this room, even if I placed it by the door.

KOKORI: (*Smiles.*) Okay, I was joking anyway. Let's go on.

JOURNALIST: Okay, Chief. I won't start with your background because we already know who you are and how you got to your present position as Chairman of Abiama. But I will quickly ask, what inspired you to run for a second term?

KOKORI: Well, I am a goal-getter, one who believes in getting the job done. For the past three years or so, as you and some of your colleagues have witnessed, we have made radical changes and reforms in the areas of administration, infrastructural development and manpower advancement. We have built roads, schools and hospitals in our communities and trained the needed manpower to manage these facilities.

JOURNALIST: (*Cutting in.*) And you're running for a second term to do more?

KOKORI: Yes. Don't forget that I have a programme and our party has a manifesto. There is a template. Above all, the essence of government is the provision of security of lives and property and to cater to the welfare of the citizens. I have to consolidate on these achievements and even do more for my people.

JOURNALIST: What makes you stand out amongst your peers and especially, your opponent?

KOKORI: (*Smiles.*) My experience, first of all, makes me thick. Mind you, I did not come from nowhere to become

Chairman of Abiama. I served as Councillor for four years before assuming duties as Chairman. My opponent has not even learnt the ropes of grassroot development. Yet, he expects to unseat me.

JOURNALIST: The opposition has condemned your household's decision, especially the decision by your wife and children to live outside of Abiama, in the city. Does this mean that Abiama is not beautiful or secure enough for your family?

KOKORI: I don't worry too much about what the opposition thinks. It's simple, my family and I lived in the city long before I became interested in Abiama politics. Our family home is there and I will move back to the city immediately I complete my constitutional two terms in office.

JOURNALIST: Why won't they live here with you, at least for the period that you're Chairman? The opposition is condemning you for keeping them there intentionally. They say that you've done this because the schools and other facilities here are not of a good enough standard to keep them in Abiama.

KOKORI: I have told you, my family house remains in the city. I will not drag the house to Abiama. My government has provided the best of schools here, comparable with those you have in the town.

JOURNALIST: Why then has your family run to the city? Can your children not school in Abiama?

KOKORI: (*Sighs heavily.*) Young lady, why are you flogging this issue? I thought you're here to better my chances at the poll? It sounds like you're speaking for the opposition. I hope you were not sponsored to bring me down.

JOURNALIST: (*Smiles.*) No, Sir.

KOKORI: Then leave my family out of your questions. In short, it may interest you to know that my wife will be here shortly, this week.

JOURNALIST: (*Cuts in.*) I know that she's only coming to cast her vote, after which she will return to the city.

KOKORI: Yes. What is wrong with it? Let us leave the details of my family out of this interview, I beg.

JOURNALIST: (*Assuredly.*) We will not go there again.

KOKORI: (*Sarcastically.*) Thank you.

JOURNALIST: Concerning the demonstration by the youths from the North-East community, the people say that you've refused to complete the North-East road and other projects around the area because of your disagreement with the former minister from the area who has been a constant critic of your administration.

KOKORI: (*Sighs.*) Eh heh, people say all sorts of things. Since the former minister comes from that area, he should complete the project. What did he do for other areas in the LG when he was minister? He should even be happy that I started the road.

JOURNALIST: There are rumours that you refused to honour the invitation of the consortium of journalists to attend the debate yesterday. Can you confirm or deny it?

KOKORI: I will do neither of both. I called the hosts of the debate and informed them of my ill health. What's the big deal? I was unwell, down with malaria. You can see that I'm just recuperating. Or is there any place in the constitution where it is written that a government official should not be ill?

JOURNALIST: And they refused to postpone?

KOKORI: Well, I don't know about that. Besides, I had a lot of work to do.

JOURNALIST: (*Cuts in.*) Are you saying that you were too busy to attend the debate or you were unwell?

KOKORI: Both. I was unwell. Yet, I had a lot to deal with on my desk.

JOURNALIST: Rumour has it that you failed to attend because the questions were not released to you before the debate.

KOKORI: (*Cutting in.*) I hope that this session is not for the clarification of rumours, because I do not dwell on tittle-tattle. I have just given you genuine reasons why I was absent from the debate. Take it or leave it.

JOURNALIST: Then you're not afraid of the opposition?

KOKORI: (*Surprised.*) How can I be afraid of my opposition? (*Giggles.*) I am the incumbent Chairman. Thus, it should be the other way round, the opposition is afraid of me.

JOURNALIST: Have you imagined coming out unsuccessful in Saturday's election?

KOKORI: (*Laughs.*) I cannot imagine such nonsense. It is not even possible. My people tell me that we are in the lead. In fact, the only reason that we still campaign is to secure the remaining ten percent of the votes to ensure total victory. Even if we go to sleep, the opposition will have no chance.

JOURNALIST: You're certain of victory then?

KOKORI: Very certain. I've done more projects than any other Chairman in recent times. (*Confidently.*) Yes.

JOURNALIST: Very well, Sir, thank you for granting this interview.

KOKORI: Thank you.

JOURNALIST: (*Switching off the recorder.*) My editor has promised that we will carry this in tomorrow's edition of our paper, with a large section dedicated to your profile and photographs of some of your projects.

KOKORI: Very good, very good. Your editor is my friend.

JOURNALIST: (*Rising*.) Let me run, Sir. I'm very sorry about the break-in. I heard this morning.

KOKORI: (*Surprised, angry*.) How? Who told you?

JOURNALIST: (*Rising*.) I heard some of your men at the gate discussing in hushed tones and I noticed that the door had been tampered with.

KOKORI: Please, do not report any of this or share the information with your colleagues. We are on top of the situation and we do not want to cause any panic.

JOURNALIST: I understand, Sir.

KOKORI: Let me get you a little token since you refused to eat in my house.

JOURNALIST: (*Contemplatively*.) Ah, no … please, don't bother, Sir.

KOKORI: Why? You don't collect gifts, too? Please, give me a minute.

(*Exit. JOURNALIST looks around. Then enter KOKORI after thirty seconds, handing her a brown envelope containing money.*)

Here. This should buy your breakfast or lunch.

JOURNALIST: (*Smiles gratefully*.) Thank you very much, Sir.

KOKORI: Thank you, too.

JOURNALIST: And good luck at the poll.

KOKORI: We have all the luck on our side. Thanks. Bye-bye.

JOURNALIST: Bye, Chief. (*Exit*.)

KOKORI: (*Calling*.) Timipa.

TIMIPA: (*Entering*.) Yes, Sir.

KOKORI: Quickly go and get a locksmith to fix this door now now.

TIMIPA: (*Without haste*.) Yes, Sir …

KOKORI: And tell those people at the gate that I do not want any information about the break-in last night to get to the public or else they lose their jobs.

TIMIPA: Yes, Sir.

KOKORI: Quickly, go.

TIMIPA: (*Hastily.*) Okay, Sir. (*Exit from main door.*)

(*Exit* KOKORI *to inner chamber. Lights fade.*)

Scene Seven

*The day before the election day. Lights. Empty stage. Then enter
KOKORI, EBITI and SALOME hastily. They all go to sit, looking
worried.*

EBITI: Your Excellency, you shouldn't worry about that small
boy.

> (KOKORI *ignores him and everyone is quiet for a minute.*)
> Who is he? He doesn't even have a solid political foundation.
> Warigbani cannot talk before you, Your Excellency. He is
> an ant.

KOKORI: (*Furious.*) Shut up, Ebiti. (*Everyone is quiet for another
minute.*) Polls open in less than twenty-four hours and you're
calling my opposition an ant?

EBITI: Certainly, Your Excellency. What would you have me call
him?

KOKORI: (*Angry.*) You are all fools. You understand nothing.
I've given you a small job. I provided you with all the
resources to execute. Yet, things start falling apart on the
eve of the election?

EBITI: (*Eargerly.*) Nothing is falling apart, Your Excellency.

KOKORI: (*Still furious, sacarstically.*) Don't give me that, Your
Excellency!

EBITI: (*Shrinking back.*) I'm very sorry, Chief. But we are still
on track.

KOKORI: (*Cuts in.*) On what track, Ebiti? All twenty-three
political parties and their leaders, whom I supported
financially in the past three and a half years, have come
out publicly to support Mr Warigbani and yet, you say that
we are on track. What track are you talking about?

EBITI: Don't worry about those parties. They are too small to make us lose sleep. Don't forget that we are still the largest political party in Africa and the opposition is an ant before you.

KOKORI: Don't make me lose my temper, Ebiti. You were supposed to lobby these parties. I've given you over eleven million to settle them. Are you telling me that they no longer need my money or did you divert those funds?

EBITI: (*Defensive.*) God forbid, Chief. Why would you say a thing like that?

SALOME: Well, Chief, I think the game is just beginning and what happened this morning shouldn't make us feel threatened by the opposition. Chief Ebiti was right in calling that guy an ant. That is exactly what he is.

EBITI: (*Nods.*) Eh eh.

SALOME: I am a woman, a strong one at that. If not the strongest in Abiama, I am one of them. I know that some of the women in my group are members of these opposition parties.

KOKORI: (*Cuts in.*) And they didn't take part in sharing my largesse?

SALOME: (*Confident.*) Chief, sometimes these women are smarter than you think. Of course, I gave them everything you asked me to. You will see what will happen tomorrow. I trust my fellow women. We will take you to the promised land.

EBITI: (*Nods*) You hear, Chief? We shouldn't worry too much about these petty political maggots.

KOKORI: (*Furious.*) Shut up, Ebiti. You are bigger than those you call ants and maggots, yet, you couldn't bring them over to my side? I am beginning to have doubts about your strategy, Ebiti. Madam Salome, if you're assuring me that your women are all on my side, then I will be patient to see what happens tomorrow.

SALOME: Yes, Chief. Those political parties drumming support for the opposition are too small to make us fail. They are, in short, insignificant, in my view. Some of them, we know already, cannot even win one vote at the council election. So, I'm not afraid of them. Their actions today will not take away more than two percent of our votes. So, let us be hopeful already. Things will work according to plan and in the end, we will pop champagne and clink glasses in this room to celebrate your victory.

KOKORI: While popping these bottles, too, I'll announce you my Special Adviser on Women Affairs. Thank you, Madam Salome.

SALOME: (*Smiles.*) Thank you, Chief.

KOKORI: We must win tomorrow's election by a wide margin. I don't care how we do it, by hook or crook. A wide margin, that's what I want.

EBITI: (*Assuredly.*) I can promise you, Chief, we will get all the votes we need for a landslide victory.

KOKORI: I hope I can count on your assurances, too, Ebiti. You cannot fail me. This election will determine where I go next after my second term. So, a landslide is not desirable. It is compulsory.

(*Enter* TIMIPA *in a hurry, looking confused.*)

TIMIPA: Chief.

KOKORI: What is it, Timipa? Can you not see that I am in a meeting?

TIMIPA: It's your phone, Sir.

KOKORI: Eh eh! What about it? Have you had my whisky again?

TIMIPA: No, Sir. It's Madam.

KOKORI: (*Angry.*) Will you speak up, Timipa? What is the problem with Madam?

TIMIPA: Someone just called from the teaching hospital to say that she was rushed in there now after sustaining injuries.

KOKORI: (*Shocked.*) What? Injuries from what? (*Rising.*)

TIMIPA: She was involved in an accident along the North-East road.

SALOME: (*Aghast.*) Jesus Christ!

EBITI: This cannot be true, Chief. Now now?

TIMIPA: Yes.

KOKORI: Who gave you this information? In fact, go inside now and get my phone.

TIMIPA: (*With haste.*) Okay, Sir. (*Exit.*)

EBITI: Please, calm down, Chief.

SALOME: This may just be the devil trying to destabilise us, Sir.

KOKORI: (*Looking at his wristwatch.*) She was supposed to arrive this morning to take part in tomorrow's election. (*Calling.*) Timipa.

TIMIPA: (*Entering.*) Here, Chief. (*Hands phone to* KOKORI.)

KOKORI: The teaching hospital?

TIMIPA: Yes, Sir.

EBITI: (*Rising.*) We are coming with you, Chief.

KOKORI: (*Confused.*) No, no, no. Ebiti and Madam, stay here. This can't be happening. (*Exit.*)

EBITI: Timipa, what happened? What did the doctor tell you?

TIMIPA: (*Sorrowfully.*) I think that Madam is dead.

EBITI: (*Shocked.*) And you didn't tell Chief?

TIMIPA: How can I break such sad news to Chief?

    (*Suddenly lights become dim.*)

SALOME: You should have informed him before he left. My God!

EBITI: The same North-East road that Chief refused to rehabilitate … Were his children in the car?

TIMIPA: The man didn't say.

EBITI: What a shame.

(*Lights fade slowly.*)

Scene Eight

Sunday, the day after the election. Lights. KOKORI's lifeless body is seen on his three-seater sofa. The sitting-room is littered with beer and whisky bottles and some dirty plates. His mobile phone rings consistently in his breast pocket for three minutes, then stops. There is a knock on the door. The knock continues for at least a minute. EBITI, SALOME and TIMIPA can be heard backstage trying to get into the room.

SALOME: Timipa, shouldn't you have another key to this door?

TIMIPA: We changed the locks on Friday. Chief is yet to give me a key.

EBITI: You're sure he's inside?

TIMIPA: He should be, Sir.

SALOME: Maybe we should leave the Chief alone. I can understand his feelings at this time.

EBITI: No. We cannot leave. I cannot imagine how that small boy rigged this election. Everyone knows that Chief won this election. He's the incumbent. We will go to court. We must. A child from nowhere, with no hard political foundation … Not possible.

SALOME: Oga Ebiti, we will not worry Chief about this yet. The man lost his wife on Friday. Now he has lost the only election that mattered to him. Maybe we should just go back and return later.

EBITI: No. Chief should call the Electoral Commissioner. I know that the sympathy he got from the people for losing his wife alone, was enough to win him this election. We should not wait another hour. Those who rigged this election must be brought to book. I trust Chief to handle this. Timipa.

TIMIPA: Sir!

EBITI: Break this door.

TIMIPA: Are you sure, Sir?

EBITI: Are you asking me? Would you break the door right away, my friend!

(*The door is hit from behind and it suddenly opens. Enter* TIMIPA, EBITI *and* SALOME, *all shocked to see* KOKORI's *lifeless body on the sofa.*)

EBITI: (*Approaching* KOKORI.) Honourable, Sir, Doctor, Chairman, Chief. (*Checking his pulse.*)

(TIMIPA *kneels on the ground, while* SALOME *goes to sit solemnly on the two-seater sofa.*)

TIMIPA: (*Places his hands on his head.*) My Chief, why?

EBITI: (*Calling sorrowfully.*) Chief, Sir, Honourable, Doctor, Chairman, Kokori Douglas, *mfr, mni, fnim.*

SALOME: (*Sorrowful.*) Indeed, the end. (*Crying.*)

(*Lights fade out slowly.*)

– CURTAIN –

Hosting Parasites

October, 2014

Characters

DR AFOLABI	—	*A civil servant in his late thirties*
DR GIWA	—	*His colleague*
OGBO	—	*Another colleague in his early thirties*
SUTU	—	*Youth corps member*
KWEEN	—	*Secretary*
SECURITY MAN		
CLEANER		
OFFICER	—	*A female vehicle licensing staff*

A radio play. The place is relatively indistinct, but the setting is
a generalised public office, and the period is fairly contemporary.

Scene One

Monday morning. At the Vehicle Licensing Office. The background noise should indicate the chaotic mood in such setting. The noise gradually disappears. A knock is heard on the door.

OFFICER: Who be dat?

DR AFOLABI: My name is Doctor Afolabi. I've come for my drivers' licence.

OFFICER: Wait small, Oga, time never reach. You no see oder people wey siddon dier dey wait?

DR AFOLABI: Please, can I just come in to ask a brief question?

OFFICER: Oga, e be like say you no hear wetin I talk before. Time never reach make we work. If you no fit wait for outside, go house.

DR AFOLABI: Please, Madam. A minute of your time and I'll leave.

OFFICER: (*Sighs.*) Which kine man be dis? Abeg, come inside, de door no close.

DR AFOLABI: Thank you.

(*SFX: Creaky door opens, closes.*)

OFFICER: Eh eh, mister man, wetin you carry come worry me this morning? I don tell you say we never open. Na because you see me here?

DR AFOLABI: Please, I understand. I have been coming here for the past two weeks to take a photograph for my licence.

OFFICER: Eh heh, the piture man never come.

DR AFOLABI: Please, Madam. That's the machine down there. Help me. I am a public servant like you.

OFFICE: (*Rude laughter.*) Oga, if na so we dey give every public servant special treatment, I for dey work twenty-four hours a day because we plentii.

DR AFOLABI: Can I sit here and wait then?

OFFICER: Oga, dat one wey you dey talk na grammar. We never open. Abeg, go wait outside.

DR AFOLABI: Can I at least have a number or write my name somewhere so that the photographer would know I came early and attend to me quickly?

OFFICER: Oga, you think say you dey America? No number. Go stay outside wait for am. He go soon come.

DR AFOLABI: It's almost eight o'clock, Madam.

OFFICER: So, wetin you want make I do?

DR AFOLABI: In fact, the clock just struck eight.

OFFICER: Na your clock be dat. Licensing Office clock never reach eight. Abeg, wait outside make I no begin vex.

DR AFOLABI: You don't have to be rude, Madam. I'm an officer, too.

OFFICER: Oya, come snap de piture yourself, Officer. Wait outside.

(*SFX: Creaky door opens and slams.*)

DR AFOLABI: What nonsense!

(*After two minutes.*)

OFFICER: Oya, Oga, begin come. Eight just nak.

(*Sound of creaky door opening and closing.*)

DR AFOLABI: Thank you.

OFFICER: Go siddon for dat chair.

DR AFOLABI: What about the man who would take the photograph?

OFFICER: Na me go do am.

DR AFOLABI: I thought you said …

OFFICER: (*Cutting in.*) Oga, you wan snap piture or not?

DR AFOLABI: Sorry, Madam. Let's get on with this.

OFFICER: I think say you never serious.

>   (*Hitting a computer.*)

DR AFOLABI: What's the problem?

OFFICER: De machine no wan start.

DR AFOLABI: Hitting it that way won't make it work either.

OFFICER: Wetin be your problem, Oga?

DR AFOLABI: Is it not a computer? I can help.

OFFICER: In fact, you don make me vex. Maybe na you carry your juju come spoil our machine dis morning. Make I go chapel go pray against principalities and powers. When I return we go take your piture.

DR AFOLABI: Ah, please, Madam. People will be waiting for me in my office.

OFFICER: Na me say make you no go your office? I no hold you o!

DR AFOLABI: Please, Madam.

>   (*Sound of Windows computer starting.*)

DR AFOLABI: I think it's coming on now.

OFFICER: Na God save you.

>   (*Operating the computer and typing on the keyboard.*)

DR AFOLABI: Ready?

OFFICER: Abeg, put your face straight.

>   (*Sound of photographic flash.*)

DR AFOLABI: Thank you.

OFFICER: We never finish.

DR AFOLABI: Oh.

OFFICER: Put you index finger here.

DR AFOLABI: Okay.

OFFICER: Your thumb.

DR AFOLABI: Okay.

OFFICER: Come next week for your licence.

DR AFOLABI: Oh, thank you very much.

OFFICER: Nothing for kola?

DR AFOLABI: What?

OFFICER: Na so dem dey do for your office?

DR AFOLABI: Are you asking me to give you a bribe?

OFFICER: Na you call am bribe o!

DR OFFICER: Really! You should be in the custody of the ICPC. Excuse me. You shouldn't even be speaking Pidgin English in a public office.

(*Sound of creaky door opening and slamming.*)

OFFICER: Sho! Na Pidgin my mama take raise me. If you no carry ICPC come collect your licence when e ready, me and you go sabi who get dis office. *Oriokpe*!

Scene Two

After fifteen minutes. At the Press and Information Unit. The sound of a key entering a keyhole and other keys dangling on the keyholder is heard. The opening and banging of the door suggest DR AFOLABI's *entry into the office.*

DR AFOLABI: (*Sighs.*) For God's sake! Why would somebody abandon a dirty plate on the table for three whole days? What is this hokum? Where are the cleaners? I've resumed before them again.

(*Lamenting.*) Something is fundamentally wrong with everyone in this country. How can everybody go home on Friday and sleep until Monday morning? Nobody works the shifts, nothing happens and everything goes. Why would the cleaners not come down here at close of work in the evenings to clean this place up before we resume in the morning? Oh, how I miss London. No one will tolerate this BS! No civilised nation will live like this. Arrant nonsense! Look.

(*The sounds of ruffling papers.*) I cannot believe these cave-minded colleagues of mine went ahead to get rid of these papers. We waste everything in this damn place. All these sheets qualify too much to be recycled.

(*Sighs.*) I wonder when we'll start doing things right.

(*Sound of door opening and closing.*)

OGBO: Ah, good morning, Doctor Afolabi. How was your weekend? Did you enjoy the match between Arsernal and Man-U yesterday?

DR AFOLABI: Please, don't greet me, Ogbonnaya. How can you people leave the office like this?

OGBO: How?

DR AFOLABI: Have you gotten so used to the mess already?

OGBO: You mean the plate on the table?

DR AFOLABI: Not just it. I asked all of you to put all these sheets in the basket over there so that they can be recycled.

OGBO: (*Laughter.*) Oga, who recycles anything in Nigeria?

DR AFOLABI: (*Not impressed.*) What do you mean?

OGBO: You're asking me … Don't you need a recycling plant first?

DR AFOLABI: No! You're going too far. Shouldn't we keep the sheets properly and use the other side to print stories before we edit them?

OGBO: Oh, I see what you mean. You too do sef, Oga Afolabi. We use the tokunbo papers sometimes, but that's when we have too many in-house documents to print. Is it because of these dirty papers that you threw my greetings back at me?

DR AFOLABI: They are dirty papers to you because you didn't buy them …

OGBO: Government did.

DR AFOLABI: And you're not part of the government?

OGBO: Doctor, no be UK you dey o! This is Nigeria and government job is no man's job. No be my papa work.

DR AFOLABI: You people will never allow us move this country forward.

OGBO: Abeg, leave that side, Doc. You don sign your name upstairs?

DR AFOLABI: I am not interested in that register you people sign upstairs. In Britain we would simply swipe our identity cards to clock in. We can't replicate such system here?

OGBO: Maybe you should have remained in the UK.

DR AFOLABI: Yes, I should have.

OGBO: Because you don't see anything good in this country anymore.

DR AFOLABI: Anything good? A country where we make the simplest things unnecessarily difficult? You should see what I experienced at the vehicle licensing office this morning to understand what I'm saying. The woman there was so blunt and rude. She even asked me for a bribe. Can you imagine? Same thing happened at NEPA on Friday, where I had gone to buy credit for my metre. The attendant there was worse.

(*Mimicking.*) 'We don't have network.' In fact, on Tuesday last week …

OGBO: (*Cutting in.*) Ah, another story? Please, don't bother, Doctor. I understand where you're heading and I agree with you. But I have to go upstairs now and write my name before they draw the line. It's almost nine o'clock.

DR: AFOLABI: Okay o!

OGBO: You sure you don't want to sign?

DR AFOLABI: What would they do with the attendance register in the end? Nothing! They're just stacking up papers that should be used to do something more important. Abeg, I'm not interested in regressivity.

OGBO: Okay. I'll be back in a jiffy.

(*SFX: Door opens and closes.*)

DR AFOLABI: OGB you're back already … Please, start work immediately on the Minister's meeting with members of the union so that we …

(*Sound of high-heeled footsteps approaching.*)

SUTU: (*Cutting in.*) Good morning, Sir.

DR AFOLABI: How are you, Sutu? Did you just come in?

SUTU: Yes. This minute.

DR AFOLABI: I thought you were OGB. Did you enjoy your weekend?

SUTU: Yes, I did, Sir. Splendid.

DR AFOLABI: Look eh, you're the most junior person in this office and I respect you because of your honesty and cleanliness.

SUTU: Oh, thank you, Sir.

DR AFOLABI: How could you have gone home on Friday without cleaning this table? You know that rats take over our desks when we go home, especially during the weekends. Yet, you left a dirty plate on the table.

SUTU: No, I didn't, Sir. I didn't come on Friday. My CDS holds on Fridays.

DR AFOLABI: Oh yes, that's true. I forgot.

SUTU: But I can clear it up, Sir.

DR AFOLABI: Oh, no problem. Just take the plate and leave it on the corridor. When the cleaners arrive, they'll take it away.

SUTU: Okay, Sir.

(There is a sharp sound of a spoon dropped in a plate.)

DR AFOLABI: You've signed upstairs?

SUTU: No. I'll do that straight away.

DR AFOLABI: Okay.

(Sounds of high-heeled footsteps leaving, door opening and closing can be heard.)

OGBO: My doctor, I have signed. Now, we can talk about Nigeria.

(Light laughter.)

DR AFOLABI: I know what I'm saying. This country is very peculiar, I tell you. The government is so insensitive and cold-blooded. They are playing tricks on us o! You people don't see it.

OGBO: Doc., you have come again. If you mean that the politicians are magicians, I concur. But politicians all over the world are the same. The American breed is not an exception.

DR AFOLABI: Yes. American politicans tell bloody lies, too. But they show some concern for their people. Here, you go to buy fuel in a jerrycan and the attendant shows you a memo from the Department of Petroleum Resources, instructing them not to sell fuel in cans. Yet, they sell in cans to those who buy kerosene. Is DPR not government? Is NEPA, too, not government? And they know that power failure is a constant phenomenon. Yet, the same government expects us to go through short cuts to get this fuel to power our generators. They know that some of these fuel attendants ask for bribes to sell in cans.

OGBO: You must know one thing, Doctor, the restrictions against selling PMS in cans is as a result of those who would sell black market petrol on the streets.

DR AFOLABI: Eh heh, why can't government arrest them? Don't you see the same touts before the NNPC headquarters, selling their wares?

OGBO: I don't understand what stops government from taking such drastic steps, though various task forces go round from time to time to arrest these touts. I also know that the sanctions against gas stations that sell to customers in jerry cans are heavy enough for them to not take the risk.

DR AFOLABI: Government was wrong to have introduced these restrictions before ensuring steady power supply in the country.

OGBO: What can they do, Sir? They've given the assurance that power failure would be a thing of the past come July.

DR AFOLABI: And you believe?

OGBO: Shouldn't I?

DR AFOLABI: Governmnet has made similar promises since the British left in 1960. You're such a young man, so you may not remember. I cannot forget in a hurry an edition of the *Daily Times* newspaper published in 1984. Guess what the headline on the front page read?

OGBO: What?

DR AFOLABI: 'NEPA: No More Blackout, 1986 Deadline.'

OGBO: (*Laughing.*) So, no be today these people begin lie.

DR AFOLABI: It's twenty-fourteen, almost thirty years after. We still have regular blackouts. And the population has multiplied since then, and demand for electricity has grown exceedingly.

OGBO: We will keep praying to God while we hope for the best, Oga.

DR AFOLABI: I'm sorry for you! You think the man up there still listens to your prayers? It is because you people pray and pray and don't use your hands to work and work that we've stayed underdeveloped. This has gone on for too long. Shouldn't we be ready to work for a better society if we hope to live in one? God will not abandon His magnificent throne in heaven to come down here to do what He has given you hands and brains to do. First, you must back your prayers up with action.

(*The sound of door opening and closing after fourteen seconds can be heard. High-heeled footsteps follow.*)

OGBO: Ah ah, Sutu, na you enter like dis?

SUTU: Good morning, Sir. I had come earlier. Went upstairs to sign. Madam is here already.

DR AFOLABI: Which Madam?

SUTU: Doctor Giwa.

DR GIWA: Chief Afolabi.

DR AFOLABI: Good morning, Ma'am. I prefer doctor. When I go to Ekiti then I'll become chief.

(*General laughter.*)

DR GIWA: A chief is a chief anywhere. Even if he goes to the moon. Unless yours is counterfeit title.

(*General laughter.*)

OGBO: Good morning, Ma. The weekend was interesting, I hope?

DR GIWA: Yeah, but it was short. Really, weekends are made in China.

(*General laughter.*)

OGBO: Doctor Afolabi was just entertaining me with his sermon on Nigeria's renaissance.

DR AFOLABI: Oh yes, Madam. You have lived in the UK before. Don't you think this country is messed up already?

DR GIWA: Doctor Afolabi, you say this every day. Yet, I haven't perceived anything that you've done to change our present situation.

DR AFOLABI: What can I do? I am an ant before these political hawks.

DR GIWA: You still believe that the fate of this nation lies only in their hands?

DR AFOLABI: Yes! Why not? Are they not the ones who control the military and the central bank? Wherever we go – left or right — they determine alone.

DR GIWA: Look, Afolabi, I expect much from you because you have a PhD. You can't think that you're not part of the government. You voted for the president in 2011. You are a federal civil servant, and most importantly, you are a citizen of this country. The little good you do in your home as its head and the little you do here in this office as a principal officer can determine a lot in the destiny of this country and change it for the better.

DR AFOLABI: No! I don't agree with you, Madam.

DR GIWA: (*Resignedly*.) Okay.

DR AFOLABI: The same government pays us so little in salaries. Yet, they have increased the pump price of petrol. The prices of beans and garri in the market have gone up. They blame it on the floods. Yet, our take-home pay hasn't changed. Government expects us to survive on this meagre sum.

DR GIWA: Yes. A good majority of our fellow countrymen are without jobs. Some who are lucky to be employed don't earn as much as you do.

DR AFOLABI: This breeds so much corruption in the system.

DR GIWA: If government wants to pay as much as you think you deserve, they'll not have the resources to spread to other vital areas of the economy.

DR AFOLABI: Why then does government employ more hands than it needs?

DR GIWA: The state is obviously a welfarist one. The national cake must go round.

SUTU: Sir, government has done well. They increased our allowee. By the time I add my allowee to the fifteen thousand I get here, believe me, I'm good to go.

DR AFOLABI: You're a corper, Sutu, plus you're a woman. You don't have many responsibilities yet. When they start coming, you will join the bandwagon.

SUTU: (*Laughs*.) Till then, Sir.

OGBO: So much poverty in the land. There, I agree with Doctor Afolabi.

DR GIWA: There's poverty everywhere. It's all over America, Europe and Asia.

DR AFOLABI: Unquestionably, Madam. But too much of it in this country. The pockets of the rich expand daily. Yet, people are hungry. The poverty rate is alarming.

DR GIWA: Afolabi, poverty is a normal condition of human beings. What government must do is increase prosperity by creating wealth. The environment must be fertile, too, to encourage private sector investment and growth. Socialism is a proven failure of wealth creation and the only place where socialism is considered successful is where it exists as a parasite on a capitalist base. Without a solid, free market, capitalistic base to provide revenue to government, socialist states are unable to remain financially viable.

OGBO: Are we a socialist state?

DR GIWA: There is no absolute capitalism or socialism anywhere in the world. So, I don't know. We move back and forth, depending on what suits us at any time. You know how a new government takes over and dumps all the projects and intiative of the former. I think we can call us a mixed economy.

DR AFOLABI: No. I think what we practise is pure thiefism.

   (*General laughter.*)

DR GIWA: Doctor, I must tell you about a natural principle that explains some of your concerns. When it rains, water doesn't remain on land. Instead, it goes back into the lakes and rivers, and all what have you.

DR AFOLABI: I don't think your analogy applies here. So, we should sit and watch our commonwealth grow only in the hands of the rich while we remain in abject poverty?

DR GIWA: Sadly so. There's very little anyone can do to change the situation.

DR AFOLABI: But you already agreed that we could, in our own little way, change the situation ... Anyway, elections are coming. We'll make the difference then.

OGBO: Have you identified a challenger yet to the incumbent?

SUTU: No opponent yet.

DR AFOLABI: The opposition parties are still working out strategies to spring up a surprise. Very soon they'll wow us with a strong candidate that will deliver us from the hands of these greedy men in power.

DR GIWA: You still think they're not all the same? Your opposition candidate would wow you negatively the moment he or she becomes president. Take it or leave it, all of them are the same, whether from the northern or southern region. Only interested in their pockets.

OGBO: Certainly, Madam. That's all politicians care about the world over.

DR AFOLABI: No. There's a little difference. Some are lesser thieves than the others and this makes a huge difference. This country is simply hosting parasites who do nothing other than take from the nation. No one is interested in giving back or sweating a dime to the country.

(*The sound of door opening and closing.*)

KWEEN: Good morning, Ma, Sirs.

DR AFOLABI: Eh heh, you're late today. Monday morning.

KWEEN: I'm sorry, Sir. My aunty compelled me to take her children to school.

DR AFOLABI: Are you telling me? Am I your employer? I was at the vehicle licensing office this morning. Yet, I got here eight twenty-seven on the dot.

DR GIWA: Doctor Afolabi, small small abeg. Give the lady a break.

DR AFOLABI: Madam, is this not what I've been saying all morning? We cannot always make excuses for our shortcomings. We are paid to work eight to four. Everybody wants a share of the national cake, yet no one wants to work for it. Parasites, that's what we all are to this nation. Very soon, we'll pay dearly for it.

DR GIWA: Yes. She's only a few minutes late. Let her settle in.

DR AFOLABI: Okay.

KWEEN: Thank you, Ma.

DR AFOLABI: Settle down and start typing the stories on your desk. Oga must receive them the moment he enters.

KWEEN: Yes, Sir.

(*After twenty seconds, KWEEN is furiously typing on the computer keyboard. After another twenty seconds, the door opens and closes. Then, the ticking sounds on the keyboard continue in a lower tone.*)

CLEANER: Good morning, Oga and Madam.

DR GIWA: Good morning. How are you?

CLEANER: I dey fine, Madam.

DR AFOLABI: (*Furiously.*) Is this when you are asked to report to work? How can I get here before you?

CLEANER: I'm very sorry, Sir. I been dey clean oga director office.

DR AFOLABI: The director resumes at nine o'clock and we resume here seven-thirty. Shouldn't you have come here first?

CLEANER: Na my supervisor say I must clean oga director office before I begin clean una own.

DR AFOLABI: Who's your supervisor?

CLEANER: Helen. She dey outside, for corridor.

DR AFOLABI: (*Angrily.*) What kind of supervisor gives such instruction? Someone needs to talk some sense into her head.

DR GIWA: Doctor Afolabi, won't you calm down?

DR AFOLABI: No, Madam.

(*Sound of door opening and closing.*)

OGBO: Madam, I think that you should talk to Doctor Afolabi. Sometimes he looses the nuts in his head.

DR GIWA: Are you saying that I'm mad, too, Ogbonnaya?

OGBO: I won't say that, Madam. You have a PhD like him, he'll understand you.

DR GIWA: My PhD is a Doctor of Philosophy. Doctor Afolabi's is a powerful high degree.

(*General laughter.*)

KWEEN: Ma, I think we should move away so that she can clean thoroughly.

DR GIWA: Oh, that's true. Please, guys, let us excuse her.

(*The computer keyboard stops clacking. Door opens and closes after thirty seconds.*)

Scene Three

Moments later. The sound of the door opening and closing is heard. Sound of high-heeled footsteps increases, then stops.

SUTU: Sir, Oga wants to see you.

DR AFOLABI: Why?

SUTU: I don't know, Sir. He just asked me to call you.

DR AFOLABI: Kween, what's keeping my story?

KWEEN: Almost done, Sir.

DR AFOLABI: Hurry up! The director has just sent for me. I'm sure he wants the story already.

KWEEN: Here, Sir. Finished.

DR AFOLABI: Thank you, Kween. Please, collect Ogbonnaya's draft as soon as he gets it ready. Get it typed and dropped on my desk. I must present it to the boss before noon.

KWEEN: Okay, Sir.

(Door opens and closes.)

OGBO: Oga Afolabi is so dedicated today.

DR GIWA: Perhaps, he visited the Queeen of England over the weekend.

(General laughter.)

OGBO: He's always dedicated on Mondays. It is the first day of work in the week.

DR GIWA: The British way of doing things hasn't departed from his system. Very soon he will get used to our style and blend with every one of us.

(Door opens and closes.)

OGBO: You've returned so soon, Doc.

DR AFOLABI: What is wrong with this man? You people must tell me.

DR GIWA: Who?

DR AFOLABI: Your director.

DR GIWA: He doesn't like the story?

DR AFOLABI: He didn't even look at it. What did you tell him, Sutu?

SUTU: Nothing, Sir.

DR AFOLABI: Then something must be going on with you two.

SUTU: What do you mean by that, Sir?

DR AFOLABI: Didn't you travel with the DG to Canada two weeks ago?

SUTU: I did.

DR AFOLABI: Guys, can you believe that Oga has again nominated Sutu to join the team travelling with the DG to Indonesia next week?

SUTU: How?

DR AFOLABI: Are you asking me? Stop pretending not to know what is going on here because you just returned from Oga's office.

SUTU: I swear. Oga didn't say anything to me about Indonesia.

DR AFOLABI: Please, don't swear to me. My Bible abhors that.

DR GIWA: Please, cut the young lady some slack, Doctor. If she says she knows nothing about this then you should believe her. Besides, Oga is the Editor-in-Chief. It is his prerogative to decide who should cover a story.

SUTU: Please, excuse me, Sir. Let me go and see Oga.

DR AFOLABI: You are excused.

(High-heeled footsteps. Door opening and closing.)

OGBO: The things we see in this office ... I thought Oga drew up a roster for all of us so that we can each travel with the DG this year?

DR GIWA: Dr Afolabi, you may have to learn how not to put your name in Oga's black book.

DR AFOLABI: What black book?

DR GIWA: How can you accuse Sutu of having an affair with Oga?

DR AFOLABI: I did not say that.

DR GIWA: It was implied. Look, news fly very fast here and you do not know who likes your face and who doesn't. Whether you approve or not, Sutu is one of Oga's favourites. Everybody knows that they are very close. To say what you've said in her presence is as good as saying it to Oga himself. Maybe you don't know that she has gone to tell him everything.

DR AFOLABI: Let her go. This is a public office and we cannot abuse public trust. Due process must be observed always. Is the young lady no longer a corps member? All of us here are confirmed staff who have each given at least four years in the service of our fatherland. Sutu just left the university yesterday and she's already travelling across the globe in the company of big boys.

OGBO: Unfortunately, Sir, this is how we live and no one can change that overnight. We just wait until it gets to our turn.

DR AFOLABI: No. We must start somewhere to tackle this problem head-on. We can't allow Sutu of all people, embark on this journey when none of us have seen the walls of the international airport this year.

OGBO: Well, do you have a plan?

(*Silence for ten seconds.*)

KWEEN: Oga Afolabi, Sutu is a woman. She is young and beautiful. Even if she doesn't run after these favours, they would naturally come to her.

DR AFOLABI: Why are the favours not running after you, Kween?

OGBO: How do you know that they are not running after her, too? Oga, you just left the shores of this country for only three years and you've lost touch with society. Didn't you grow up in Nigeria?

DR AFOLABI: Look, I went to primary school in Badagry, secondary school in Ogbomosho. I studied for my first degree in Ife. So, what are you talking about?

DR GIWA: Afolabi, Ogbonnaya has said the truth. It's been very obvious since you returned. You no longer understand the system.

DR AFOLABI: Madam, there is no point arguing with you people because all of you think we are in a hopeless situation and can't do anything meaningful to change our lot. How can we know what is wrong and do nothing about it because we think the system is programmed to run that way? My professor friend in Canada will tell you that this is the reason why babies born in Nigeria to Nigerians of Nigeria scream a decibel and half louder than babies born elsewhere. It is no fun signing up for a lifetime of indignity and non-human existence. Everyone around here has acclamatised to the rot in the system. No one wants to fight or do anything to salvage the situation.

OGBO: Well, you behaved like you had a plan, Sir. Do something, we'll tag along.

DR AFOLABI: Only a matter of time. You wait and see.

(*Sound of a hard knock on the door.*)

OGBO: Enter.

(*The door opens and closes. Enter* SECURITY MAN.)

SECURITY MAN: Good morning, Sir. I say make I come tell you say I don wash your car finish.

OGBO: Oh, thank you.

SECURITY MAN: No problem, Sir.

OGBO: Take something for breakfast.

SECURITY MAN: Thank you, Sir. Nobody go block your motor today as far as I dey there.

OGBO: Thank you, my brother.

(*Door opens and is shut.*)

DR AFOLABI: Was that not a bribe you gave him?

OGBO: No. That was a tip.

DR AFOLABI: For what?

OGBO: For washing my car.

DR AFOLABI: That was clearly a bribe. Don't give it a beautiful name to cover your face.

OGBO: See me see wahala. There is a thin line between a bribe and a gift. Where and how do you draw that line? Please, tell me, Sir, you have a PhD.

DR AFOLABI: Each time I ask that man to wash my car, an excuse will just fall from heaven. Now he didn't only wash your car, but has assured you that no one will park another car in front of yours. Is it not because of the bribe you handed him?

(*General laughter.*)

OGBO: May God deliver us from these British people o. No wonder. The security man told me about you, that you sent him to the bank last week without transport money. You didn't hand him a little change when he returned to at least show appreciation.

DR AFOLABI: But I thanked him.

OGBO: Sometimes thank you isn't enough.

DR AFOLABI: Anyway, I do not give bribes. I wasn't trained to be corrupt.

OGBO: (*Laughter.*) Don't worry, Doctor. If you were not trained that way, the harsh conditions in this town will teach you.

DR AFOLABI: Till then. (*Silence for a minute.*) How is the story coming?

OGBO: There! It's finished. I took it from the minister's angle.

DR AFOLABI: Fair enough. (*Calling.*) Kween!

KWEEN: Sir!

DR AFOLABI: Take this document. Start typing immediately. I will take it to Oga in twenty minutes. That's if he bothers to look at it.

KWEEN: Okay, Sir.

(*Door opens and slams. High-heeled footsteps.*)

DR AFOLABI: Sutu, you will cover the event happening at the City Council secretariat on Friday. The Secretary to the Government of the Federation and the Minister will be there.

SUTU: I'm sorry, Sir. You know I will be too busy preparing for my trip to Indonesia. Besides, my CDS is …

DR AFOLABI: (*Cutting in.*) I thought you knew nothing about Indonesia?

SUTU: Yes. I just returned from Oga's office. He has informed me.

DR AFOLABI: And you're happy?

SUTU: I don't know, Sir. Should I not be?

DR AFOLABI: (*Pulling a chair.*) Sit down, young lady.

SUTU: Thank you, Sir.

DR AFOLABI: Don't thank me yet. Let me advise you because I know that nobody around here would be very blunt with you. You are still very young and you have many years ahead of you. Do you want to ruin your chances at marriage?

SUTU: How do you mean, Sir?

DR AFOLABI: People are saying that you're having an affair with the director.

SUTU: What? God forbid, Sir. Who said that? The man is older than my father.

DR AFOLABI: Please, let us not make so much noise about this.

SUTU: Who gave you such callous information, Sir? I want to know because it is capable of dragging me into a scandal.

DR AFOLABI: Don't worry about my source. You're a journalist, too, and you know how it is in the profession.

SUTU: This is not journalism, Sir. This is about my name. It is defamatory. In fact, scandalous.

DR AFOLABI: Sutu, you shouldn't be seen in the company of old men. I'm not interested in the salt of this rumour. But keep yourself intact so that your would-be husband would be proud. You don't know who carries the virus. People don't have it written on their heads.

SUTU: Sir, please, I have taken your advice because I respect you. But it is not necessary because the story is a lie, a big one.

OGBO: Excuse me.

DR AFOLABI: Excuse you for what?

OGBO: I burped.

DR AFOLABI: All right. You're excused, Ogbonnaya. Don't disturb my interaction with the young lady.

SUTU: That is all, Sir, I hope.

DR AFOLABI: Yes. Stay away from these men. They are not interested in your success. They just want to hold you for a moment and dump you when they're finished. Someone may be watching you with the intention of marring you. And because he sees you with Oga, he may back off, thinking you are rotten. But I know you are as good as you look. So, don't let a man who is already married ruin your chances of finding a spouse.

SUTU: I've taken your advice, Sir.

DR AFOLABI: So, about the story for Friday ...

SUTU: I told you, Sir, I have to run here and there to process my visa. As I heard, the note verbal is already being prepared. I also have to get myself ready for the trip.

DR AFOLABI: I understand, Sutu. But you must be engaged in one way or another this week. You are the most junior officer here. We can't continue covering your beats.

SUTU: Just this one time, Sir, please. I don't want to be engaged in very serious assignments so that I don't disappoint you guys.

DR AFOLABI: Okay. You have your way this week. Nevertheless, we expect multiple stories from you if you go to Indonesia.

SUTU: No problem, Sir. The drafts will be ready on your desk immediately we return.

DR AFOLABI: Good.

SUTU: Can I be excused, please? I want to go to the chapel to say my prayers.

DR AFOLABI: Didn't you just say you wouldn't want to be engaged in serious activities? Haven't you done this enough already, Sutu?

SUTU: Praying to God is never enough, Sir. We keep thanking and praising Him as long as we have breath in us.

DR AFOLABI: (*Resignedly.*) Okay. You can go.

SUTU: Thank you, Sir.

(Moving chair. High-heels walking away. Door opens and closes. General laughter.)

KWEEN: Oga Afolabi don see the one wey pass him power.

DR AFOLABI: Don't disturb me, Kween. Face your work.

DR GIWA: Hian! Dr Afolabi, it will take you some five years to readapt to this country. You're not even afraid that Sutu will go back to Oga and tell him that you asked her to stay away from him.

DR AFOLABI: That doesn't bother me. It wasn't a bad advice.

OGBO: Oga, no one has said that your advice is bad. However, you should look before you leap.

(Telephone rings.)

DR GIWA: Hello, Press and Information Unit. *(Silence.)* Nobody here by that name. Hold on … Doctor Afolabi, this lady has called for a Mister Akinlabi. It sounds much like yours.

DR AFOLABI: Where is she calling from?

DR GIWA: Give me a sec, let me find out. Hello, please, where are you calling from? Oh, protocol.

DR AFOLABI: Please, let me speak to her.

(Silence.)

Yes, Doctor Afolabi speaking.

(He is silent for eleven seconds.)

Wait a minute. Oga just informed us that Sutu will be the one making the trip … She has gone to the chapel … I'll ask her to see you when she returns.

(Sound of phone receiver slaming down.)

Can you imagine, Oga?

DR GIWA: What?

DR AFOLABI: He subsititued my name for Sutu's.

OGBO: For the trip?

DR AFOLABI: What else? Am I not her senior in all ramifications? On what grounds should he do that and what gives him the right?

DR GIWA: Simple! He likes the young lady. Plus, he is your director.

DR AFOLABI: This is unacceptable, Madam.

DR GIWA: Go and tell him.

DR AFOLABI: I won't. But I'll report him immediately to the DG.

(*General laughter.*)

DR GIWA: Unless you don't like your seat. Do that and you will be forced into redundancy.

DR AFOLABI: No way! Nobody has the right to do that. You forget we are civil servants.

DR GIWA: And you forget that it would only take a memo to move you to a department where you'll be idle for the rest of your bloody life and regret ever getting a PhD.

DR AFOLABI: He can't do that. It is utterly wrong and does not concur with the public service rules.

DR GIWA: So are you going to the DG to report your boss?

(*Sound of Christian praise and worship in a very low tone.*)

DR AFOLABI: Can you hear that?

DR GIWA: What?

DR AFOLABI: Sutu and her people.

DR GIWA: Yes. They make all that noise whenever they prepare for lent. Today marks the first day of lent.

DR AFOLABI: We live in a very funny society. Everyone wants to pray all the time. What kind of prayer are Sutu and her fellow worshippers making there that couldn't have been done at home?

DR GIWA: It is allowed. Government built that chapel.

DR AFOLABI: I know, with taxpayers' money. We can't allow people to continue using the time they should work for government to do private things. These things will not happen in private companies.

DR GIWA: Welcome to the public service. Such things are very much permitted.

DR AFOLABI: It's nonsense!

OGBO: Yet, no one can stop it. We live in a very religious society. The Muslims must say their prayers five times a day, the Christians, too, whenever they wish. Haven't you travelled around the city lately? All government offices seem to now have chapels and mosques. This is because government respects our right to congregate to worship God.

DR AFOLABI: At its expense?

OGBO: Yes. It is these prayers that maintain the balance between the spiritual and physical realm.

DR AFOLABI: All rubbish. I will demolish these structures when I'm president.

DR GIWA: By coup or by votes?

DR AFOLABI: Votes, of course.

DR GIWA: People will reject an uptight man like you. You are too strict in reality.

DR AFOLABI: Strict is what the country needs right now.

DR GIWA: People don't need a man who will demolish their places of worship.

DR AFOLABI: People don't know what they need. They don't understand governance. This is why you find old women waiting and dancing on the streets when a governor or president travels to commission a petty project such as a water borehole or a town's market. I will never commission such projects as president or governor. Those projects should be executed by the local government and commissioned by its chairman. The majority of us are illiterates. We do not know what we want and don't want. God help you people in this country o!

DR GIWA: You're in this country, too. God help you.

DR AFOLABI: Two churches in my estate tried to outsmart each other with their loudspeakers some Sundays ago. I live over five hundred metres away. Yet, I heard all their noises.

DR GIWA: Typical. We hear them everywhere.

DR AFOLABI: There's nothing normal about it. We can't all go mad and assume that an abnormality should make part of our daily living.

DR GIWA: We can do nothing about them. Their worship is to God.

DR AFOLABI: No. Lagos governor has dealt with this menace in his state. For me, I wrote to the facility managers of my estate and they stopped these churches from placing their speakers outside. I shouldn't be forced to listen to their sermons. Such gibberish is not tolerated in the UK.

OGBO: You called it the UK, Sir. We cannot always be like the UK.

DR AFOLABI: They colonised us.

OGBO: OYO is your case then.

DR AFOLABI: What's that?

KWEEN: You're on your own, Sir.

DR AFOLABI: Oh! (*General laughter.*) What a country. I hope God answers the prayers of Sutu and her fellows.

DR GIWA/KWEEN: Amen.

(*The thwack of a newspaper on the table can be heard.*)

DR AFOLABI: Look at today's headline. Twenty-two killed by insurgents in Borno. Another one, attacks by Fulani herdsmen claim thirty lives in Benue and Taraba States. *The Sun* reports another bloodbath in the Niger Delta as militants clash, claiming twelve lives. This is heartbreaking and outrageous. Everywhere blood, blood, blood. People no longer have regard for human life. Look at this report.

(*Reading from a newspaper.*)

Witnesses described Boko Haram laying siege to towns, villages and highways, looting and burning houses, shops and vehicles, and executing and decapitating people. Hear the leader of the insurgents too: 'I enjoy killing anyone that God commands me to kill, the way I enjoy killing chickens and rams!' How can anyone make such statements?

OGBO: Oga, don't worry yourself. Since the international community has vowed to intervene, all these killings will be a thing of the past.

DR AFOLABI: By that time a lot of lives would have been lost.

OGBO: What else can we do?

DR AFOLABI: A peaceful break-up. Let all ethnic groups go their way.

DR GIWA: All two hundred and fifty?

DR AFOLABI: Yes. After all, the US predicted that we won't be together beyond twenty-fifteen.

DR GIWA: A myopic prediction. It relied heavily on the fact that the Nigerian almagamation treaty, signed between the northern and southern protectorate, was for an initial hundred years. It's already a hundred years. We're marching forward.

DR AFOLABI: Forward to where? With all these killings happening here and there? The only solution is a peaceful separation.

DR GIWA: You shouldn't forget that you have a PhD, Doctor Afolabi. When someone qualified as you are, suggests to others that the country should split ethnically, one begins to think that all hope is lost. The problems that we face in the country today have no business with ethnicity or religion. Obviously, the demarcation is between the rich and the poor. Watch the *owambe* parties on television and those on the glossy pages of magazines. Are they not attended by rich men and women from all parts of the country? They assemble every time to suppress you and I, and knock our heads together. Later, they go to the pages of newspapers to make religious, north and south dichotomy arguments that give us the impression that our problem lies in these differences. I don't expect someone in your position to fall into that trap.

OGBO: I know that we will not break up anyway. We cannot. We've become too mature to even consider it. And I know for sure that it wouldn't do us any good. Go and read Obii Okwelume's book, *Babel of Voices*. It says it all. We lose everything the moment we consider a separation, peaceful or violent.

DR AFOLABI: Oh fine, we will not break. What then is the solution? We can't continue living like this.

KWEEN: I think we must tackle corruption squarely before any other thing.

DR AFOLABI: You mean the government?

DR GIWA: No. All of us. We are all responsible for our problems. If we always do what is expected of us to the best of our abilities, we'll begin to witness some positive changes around the country. But as long as everyone sits and expects government alone to act, we won't move away from here.

DR AFOLABI: In other words, the followership is as much the problem as the leadership …

DR GIWA: Exactly.

OGBO: We've not made the best decision to borrow the governance structures of the West. We *zeroxed* their system and threw away our original forms of governance, which were in themselves, more appropriate. The sociopolitical life of the Igbo ethnic group, for instance, has always involved a representative principle, call it democracy if you like. This life is conducted by numerous groups, including the nuclear family, the extended ones and other groups. A unique illustration of this representative governing system is in the town unions, a group more powerful than the traditional council of chiefs in some areas like my town. Primarily, they exist to promote development for the townspeople and coordinate other political, social issues. Because they have branches scattered in several towns across the country where every adult indigene is allowed membership, the branches conduct debates when decisions that will affect the town is considered. All members, irrespective of age or status, are allowed to speak no matter what. A decision is taken and reported back to headquarters, usually in the town. Then a final decision is taken based on the presentations of the various branches and EXCO members in headquarters. In short, town unions are the congresses of the towns and village groups. They have the responsibility of writing and upholding the town's constitution. The British didn't teach us to operate this way. The system was well in place before they invaded us. So we don't have to dwell so much on their forms of governance. Each ethnic group in Nigeria has a unique governance style and I believe we must absorb them now by tapping into the goodness and vitality that they bring.

DR GIWA: I think so, too. We have a lot to take from our tradition.

DR AFOLABI: We can't disagree on that. But we have a lot to learn from the British, too.

(*Door opens, closes. High-heeled footsteps can be heard.*)

SUTU: Oga, I am back, Sir.

DR AFOLABI: You pray too long.

DR GIWA: Afolabi … Free Sutu small jor.

SUTU: (*Laugh.*) It's the season, Sir. I want to go and put something in my stomach.

DR AFOLABI: Haba! I thought you people said that this is the period of lent?

SUTU: Yes. We just started. It'll take my body sometime to get used to it. Until then.

DR GIWA: Sutu, don't mind Doctor Afolabi. Go and have your breakfast.

SUTU: (*Softly.*) Okay, Ma. Thank you.

(*Sound of high-heels walking away and door opening and closing can be heard.*)

DR AFOLABI: Comedy all over the place. Has Sutu not gallivanted since she came in this morning? From Oga's office to church, now food? Okay! Make we dey watch how una wan change dis country.

(*General laughter.*)

KWEEN: We will be fine, Oga, no worry.

DR AFOLABI: Me, I'm not worried o! Make I come begin go bank.

DR GIWA: You see yourself. You're complaining about another's crime and you're doing the exact same thing.

DR AFOLABI: Madam, our people ask us to behave like the Romans when we're in Rome.

(*General laughter.*)

Make I run. I dey come now now. Abeg, if Oga asks about me, I dey toilet. I can tell him that I took purgative last night.

OGBO: Okay, Sir.

(*A trash can is knocked over.*)

KWEEN: Ah, take am easy, Oga Afolabi, abeg.

DR AFOLABI: Sorry, Kween. Abeg, pick it up later.

KWEEN: No problems, Sir.

(*Door opens and slams.*)

Scene Four

Afternoon. At the car park. Wind builds. Footsteps stomping the ground. DR AFOLABI *whistles for ten seconds.*

DR AFOLABI: Today, my lucky day.

(*Wind stops blowing,* OGBO's *car drives up.*)

OGBO: My oga, I'm going to the bank, too. You wanna join me?

DR AFOLABI: Ah, no, thank you, my brother. I must go in my car.

OGBO: Okay. Thought you'd want to save your fuel.

DR AFOLABI: No. Thanks for the gesture.

OGBO: My pleasure.

(*Car horns, driving away. Footsteps continue. Car door opens and closes. Car driving through most parts of the scene.* DR AFOLABI *is playing a Yoruba gospel compact disc in his car. After a minute, music stops and switches to a Westlife love track. Car pulls up. High-heeled footsteps, slowly moving.*)

DR AFOLABI: Hello, Sutu, going my way?

SUTU: (*Surprised.*) Ah, you found me, Doctor Afolabi.

DR AFOLABI: I have eyes for good things.

SUTU: Which way are you heading?

DR AFOLABI: Anywhere you're heading.

SUTU: Are you sure, Sir? I don't want to be a distraction.

DR AFOLABI: No, you won't. I'm at your service. Hop in.

SUTU: Okay, Sir.

(*Car door opens and closes, then driving. Music volume reduces. External noises – other cars, horns, people, etc.*)

DR AFOLABI: Wind up, let us drive with the air conditioner.

SUTU: Okay.

(*External noises disappear.*)

DR AFOLABI: Where are you heading actually?

SUTU: Sheraton.

DR AFOLABI: Like seriously?

SUTU: (*Smiles.*) Noooo. I was pulling your legs. I eat at the bukka down the road.

DR AFOLABI: I could drive up to Sheraton if that's where you want to eat.

SUTU: No, Sir. It's expensive there.

DR AFOLABI: Call me Afolabi, I'm not Sir.

SUTU: Okay, Sir… Afolabi.

DR AFOLABI: Sheraton it is. I'll pay.

SUTU: Are you sure about that, Sir?

DR AFOLABI: Damn sure, young lady.

SUTU: Wow. I've never had lunch in such big hotels.

DR AFOLABI: Oh no, it's nothing. While I was abroad, I had breakfast in Sheraton, lunch in the Marriott and dinner in the Grand Hyatt. There I was regaled with every kind of delicacy.

SUTU: Wow.

DR AFOLABI: These days hotels haven't been my thing. The local hotels here are not good enough for me. But we can do Sheraton. I can manage.

SUTU: Thank you, Sir.

DR AFOLABI: I asked you not to call me that.

SUTU: I'm sorry.

DR AFOLABI: It's okay.

SUTU: You like Westlife?

DR AFOLABI: Yeah, that's all I listen to.

SUTU: Wow, looks like you're very young at heart.

DR AFOLABI: And of body and looks, too. I'm not as old as you think. Forget about the little grey hair on my head and chin. They all erupted when I was writing my PhD thesis.

SUTU: It was the stress, I guess.

DR AFOLABI: Yes. What are your plans for life after NYSC – marriage, postgraduate degree or just work?

SUTU: I'm confused right now. But I want to wait until I've concluded this stage of my life. I'm open to suggestions, though.

DR AFOLABI: Okay. I can assist you in getting an offer to do a PG degree in the UK. I'll call up the vice-chancellor of my university. He's a close friend.

SUTU: You'll do that for me?

DR AFOLABI: Why not? We are here already.

SUTU: Yes.

(*Music stops. Car doors open and close.*)

DR AFOLABI: After you.

SUTU: Thank you.

DR AFOLABI: Let's sit at the bar and have a drink first.

SUTU: Okay.

DR AFOLABI: Chapman for the lady and extra stout for me.

SUTU: That's exactly what I take when I'm not having Smirnoff Ice.

DR AFOLABI: I could guess.

(*Sound of bottles and glasses.*)

SUTU: Thanks.

DR AFOLABI: What about your parents?

SUTU: They live in Lagos.

DR AFOLABI: Who's keeping you here?

SUTU: My uncle. He is married to my big cousin.

DR AFOLABI: He's your in-law.

SUTU: Yeah.

DR AFOLABI: I hope you don't mind that I'm difficult sometimes at the office. We do these things sometimes to get the job done and meet up with deadlines.

SUTU: I understand, Sir.

DR AFOLABI: Don't sir me again.

SUTU: (*Light laughter.*) I'm very sorry.

DR AFOLABI: What do you want to eat?

SUTU: Well, for starters, vegetable soup with pasta and a drizzle of pesto. Then creamy rice with forest mushrooms … Custard profiteroles with chocolate sauce or caramelised and flambéed pineapple with vanilla ice cream for dessert.

DR AFOLABI: You would eat all that?

SUTU: (*Laughs lightly.*) Yes. It's not as heavy as it sounds.

DR AFOLABI: Oh.

SUTU: But I have to return to the office soon. Protocol woman asked me to see her at two-thirty.

DR AFOLABI: Oh, good. We can leave now.

SUTU: Oh yes.

DR AFOLABI: Maybe dinner some other time …

SUTU: Not a bad idea.

DR AFOLABI: Let me pay the bartender.

SUTU: Okay.

(*A cash register bell rings.*)

DR AFOLABI: Thank you. Keep the change.

(*Sound of high-heeled footsteps and howling wind.*)

SUTU: It would rain heavily.

(*Car door opens and closes. Wind stops.*)

DR AFOLABI: Right. The weather is just perfect for two.

SUTU: It's definitely going to rain.

DR AFOLABI: You didn't hear me?

SUTU: What?

DR AFOLABI: Forget it.

(*Car engine coming on. Westlife music comes on for five seconds and is turned off.*)

SUTU: Why did you switch off the radio?

DR AFOLABI: I'm not in the mood.

SUTU: Oh yes, the weather is perfect for couples.

DR AFOLABI: You think so, too?

SUTU: Yeah.

DR AFOLABI: You know I've always thought you were the most beautiful thing on this planet.

SUTU: And you've never mentioned?

DR AFOLABI: Em, you know how it is.

SUTU: Okay.

DR AFOLABI: I like you, though.

SUTU: Is that why you treat me with so much disdain?

DR AFOLABI: Awwww, you should have known I was only trying to get your attention.

SUTU: You got it now.

DR AFOLABI: I know.

> (*There is a crash of thunder. Then, silence for thirty seconds.*)

You know we can go to a cool spot and relax. The weather is perfect.

SUTU: Oh yeah.

DR AFOLABI: So what do you say?

SUTU: What do I say?

DR AFOLABI: We go to the guest house by the bukka.

SUTU: To do what?

DR AFOLABI: You know what … Why are you starting to behave like a child?

SUTU: Excuse me, Sir. Is that what this kindness is about? FYI, I'm not that kind of girl.

DR AFOLABI: Ah ah, but you see the director behind us. You think I don't know? You don't want me to chop from the same plate as Oga, abi?

SUTU: I beg your pardon, Sir. You think I'm a prostitute? I don't sleep around. Besides, AIDS is real.

DR AFOLABI: Why are you pretending, Sutu? What's the big deal? Am I not younger and better looking than Oga?

SUTU: Oga is my uncle. He is married to my big cousin.

DR AFOLABI: Oga is the same uncle you live with?

SUTU: Yes.

DR AFOLABI: How come nobody knows?

SUTU: Do I have to explain my relationships to everybody?

DR AFOLABI: Little wonder he always favoured you with official trips.

SUTU: I don't know about that, Sir. Please, take me back to the office.

(*Silence for at least thirty seconds.*)

DR AFOLABI: Please, don't tell anyone about this.

SUTU: What?

DR AFOLABI: That I took you out for lunch.

SUTU: Did you?

DR AFOLABI: Well, for a couple of drinks.

SUTU: Don't worry yourself. Just pray that nobody sees me alighting from your car when we get to the office.

DR AFOLABI: I have an idea.

SUTU: What idea?

DR AFOLABI: I won't drive with you into the office premises. I'll stop before the gate so that you get off and go to the office while I park. Please.

SUTU: No problems. Drop me off here.

DR AFOLABI: Okay.

(*Sound of car stopping and door opening.*)

SUTU: Thank you sir.

(*Sound of car door closing.*)

DR AFOLABI: Kai! Not my lucky day, after all.

OFFICER: Stop there, mister man! Where you dey go?

DR AFOLABI: (*Angry.*) Woman, would you vamoose before I render your body lifeless with my car.

OFFICER: Oh, na me you wan take this nonsense hit? Oya, park well, park well.

DR AFOLABI: What is the meaning of this, Officer? I'm right in front of my office.

OFFICER: Wetin concern me? Park well, my friend!

DR AFOLABI: For what? What offence have I committed?

OFFICER: Wrong parking!

DR AFOLABI: I just parked to drop a colleague.

OFFICER: I see when you drop am na. You too follow like women.

DR AFOLABI: Are you not the same woman I met at the vehicle licensing office this morning?

OFFICER: Oh, na you! Mister ICPC. This world small no be small. God don throway you for my doormot again. E don catch you!

DR AFOLABI: Please, Madam. This is where I work. I told you that I am a civil servant like you.

OFFICER: Civil servant? Oga, park that motor well, come down.

DR AFOLABI: Madam, I don't want to cause any trouble, please.

OFFICER: You wan tell me say you be trouble-maker, abi? Carry all your particulars come down.

DR AFOLABI: Please, Madam, can't I just apologise and go? We are right before my office.

OFFICER: Oga, if na apology we dey collect from traffic offenders like you, government for no see money chop. You think say na apology government take sew my uniform? Na money! Abeg, come down, no waste government time!

DR AFOLABI: Please.

OFFICER: Mustapha, oya, park that van for this man front. He no wan cooperate.

(A towing van moves back, towards DR AFOLABI's *car.)*

DR AFOLABI: Why are you doing this, Madam? We don't have to be this uncivilised, please.

OFFICER: Uncivilised, eh? I sure say people like you no dey pay tax to government. You want everything free.

DR AFOLABI: I pay my taxes to the FIRS directly from the source of my salary.

OFFICER: Oya, park well and show me your papers. In fact, come down and identify yourself.

DR AFOLABI: I beg you, Madam…

OFFICER: (*Cuts in.*) You still dey beg? Oya …

(*Sound of car door opening and slamming.*)

DR AFOLABI: Please, Madam.

OFFICER: You no even wear seat belt.

DR AFOLABI: I just pulled it out now because I was right in front of my office.

OFFICER: Oga, dat one na super story. De law talk say you must wear your seat belt any time you dey steering and you dey drive, until you park, whether you dey in front of your office or you dey for back.

DR AFOLABI: Okay! I am very sorry, Madam.

OFFICER: Na sorry I wan chop? If you no wan begin settle, we go tow your motor go office. Once we reach there, we go impound this motor for twenty-four hours and you go pay fine for one, driving without wearing seat belt. And two, wrong parking. All of them, forty thousand!

DR AFOLABI: Ah, Madam! Where do you expect me to get that kind of money? I am just a civil servant, not a politician.

OFFICER: And you dey drive this kine motor? No be all of una get all the houses for Abuja? My friend, begin settle.

DR AFOLABI: Please, Madam.

OFFICER: Mustapha, begin pull this man motor. Why you dey waste time?

(*The sound of the towing van's engine increases and decreases in volume.*)

DR AFOLABI: Okay, Madam. What do you want me to do?

OFFICER: As things are now, two things are involved.

DR AFOLABI: Okay.

OFFICER: You settle us here or we carry you go office to settle government.

DR AFOLABI: So what's the difference if I'm going to settle after all?

OFFICER: You no sabi? Okay, wetin you get for body now?

DR AFOLABI: I don't understand you.

OFFICER: You still dey talk as you behave this morning?

DR AFOLABI: Are you asking me for a bribe?

OFFICER: Eh heh, call am anything you wan call am. If you no pay am here, you go pay am for office. If you pay us here now now, we go give you big discount. Plus, we no go impound your motor.

DR AFOLABI: What do you want?

OFFICER: Bring half.

DR AFOLABI: Twenty thousand naira? I don't have that kind of money.

OFFICER: Wetin you get?

DR AFOLABI: You know what, Madam, if I had behaved myself this afternoon, I wouldn't have found myself in this mess, arguing with you. So I'd choose your second option. It's the right thing to do.

OFFICER: Oh, you wan go office?

DR AFOLABI: Yes. Please, take me to your office.

OFFICER: Oya, Mustapha, begin tow dis motor. Mister ICPC no dey settle. He wan go office.

(The sound of the towing van's engine can be heard. Van is connected to DR AFOLABI's car, then starts driving.)

DR AFOLABI: I hope you're happy now. Thank you.

OFFICER: No thank me o! Until we reach office. You no get shame at all for your body. Common twenty kay you no fit drop. Make we reach office, you go see wetin government go charge you. *Oriokpe*!

(Sound of the towing van driving away.)

– CURTAIN –

The Sudden Return

January, 2010

Characters

STAGE A

PAPA	—	*Old man and Nwapa's grandfather*
JOHN-CAMPBELL	—	*A man in his twenties, also called Nwapa*
MISS MANDY	—	*John-Campbell's fiancée*
MADAM DO-GOOD	—	*Papa's neighbour*
EJIKE	—	*Madam Do-Good's husband*
ELDER TIMOTHY	—	*Papa's friend*

STAGE B

NWAKAEGO	—	*A widow*
MAZI	—	*A retired civil servant*
NGOZI	—	*Mazi's new wife*
CHINEME	—	*Mazi's daughter*
EZIGBO	—	*Chineme's husband*

The stage for this play is divided into two equal parts, stages A and B. Stage A is on the left side with one entrance and exit on the wall opposite the audience. On the right side is stage B. Stage B may have two doors, one can serve as an exit and the other as an entrance. Both stages must have their own lighting systems as they may depict different locations in the different scenes. Stage A is PAPA's house and remains so throughout the play. Stage B depicts the flashbacks in the play. The place is a village in Eastern Nigeria; contemporary times.

Scene One

JOHN-CAMPBELL, *an engineer of about 29 years, has been in the United States of America for over fifteen years. He has just returned to Nigeria with his fiancée,* MISS MANDY, *whom he leaves in Lagos to travel to Eastern Nigeria to meet his grandfather and uncle concerning their marriage.*

Stage A: In PAPA's *parlour. Morning. The only audible sounds are the cutting of a tree backstage which suddenly stops after thirty seconds and those of birds which come and go intermittently. Bright lights come on stage. The room looks old. The furniture depicts the age of its owner,* PAPA, *an old man in his seventies. A three-seater armchair facing the audience and another single one adjacent it are seen at the centre of the stage. A small wooden table also sits at the centre of the stage, just in front of the chairs. Old wooden frames can be seen on the walls, holding family photographs. Some local almanacs, too, are on the wall. Enter* PAPA. *He is wearing a white singlet and tying a wrapper just below his pot belly. He also has a wristwatch strapped to his left wrist. His hair is all white, his eyebrows, too. Some grey hairs stick out from his ears and nose. He enters with a box of snuff in his left hand and sits comfortably on the three-seater chair. He spreads his legs apart and folds part of his wrapper in between them. Leaning forward, he opens his snuff box and puts some in his nose and rubs a little on his teeth. He inhales it slowly while gnashing his teeth and leans back in the chair. He places his right leg on the centre table and is quiet for a minute or two. Then, enter* JOHN-CAMPBELL. *He walks in through the door and stops for a while to yawn. He is wearing an English pyjamas and a pair of rubber slippers on his feet. He has a mobile phone in his breast pocket. He walks to the centre of the stage, close to* PAPA.

JOHN-CAMPBELL: (*With an American accent which he uses*

throughout the play.) Good morning, Papa.

(*He sits down on the single armchair.*)

Had a good night?

PAPA: (*Leaning a bit forward.*) You're up already.

JOHN-CAMPBELL: (*Nodding his head, sarcastically.*) Yeah, thanks to the mosquitoes.

PAPA: (*Giggles.*) Ah, you will get used to them. I had a very good night myself. Who wouldn't?

(*He drops his snuff box on his chair and takes his leg down from the centre table.*)

I haven't set eyes on you for more than a decade. You people abandoned me after your parents died. I have stayed on my own, lonely.

(*With mock sarcasm.*)

Even when I have grandchildren scattered in the Americas.

JOHN-CAMPBELL: (*With all seriousness, he leans a bit forward.*) The story didn't go exactly that way, Papa. We had to contend with a lot of drama in the States.

PAPA: (*Nodding his head.*) Indeed! I knew you had some problems there.

JOHN-CAMPBELL: Yeah! We couldn't accompany my folks' corpses to Nigeria because we had issues with our American passport. We lost our Nigerian passport so that was not an option. It expired, and we never had plans to return to this country.

PAPA: (*Surprised.*) Is that so?

JOHN-CAMPBELL: Yes, Papa.

PAPA: (*Still shocked.*) And my son agreed to this plan?

JOHN-CAMPBELL: Dad didn't have a choice. Each time he visited this village, he came back to the States a sad man. Problems here and there. Demands came from every angle. Mum even had to send him over two thousand dollars at one point because he had given out all the money he came to Nigeria with.

PAPA: (*Disappointed.*) Oh! You know the feeling our people get when you people return home. The feeling that Nigerians abroad live in heaven doesn't help you much, because people expect so much from you. And you know how the big boys who come from America and Europe behave ... they go around sharing dollars and showing off, giving our people the impression that people in America pluck money from trees. Yet, I know that some of these boys do not have the best jobs there. They save so much money while there for years and come down here to squander all of it in one week. This is why people expect so much from you when you return.

JOHN-CAMPBELL: I can understand that. But that's not all ... Dad used to tell us about a house he was putting up in Lagos, because he planned for us to return home someday. He talked about building a prototype of the same building here in the village once the one in Lagos was completed. But that never happened. I remember, he came home one Christmas to discover that the house he believed was his, for over three years, belonged to a general, a military general. The contractor deceived him. He squandered all the money Dad sent him from the States. This got Dad and Mum really angry. They vowed never to return to this village or Nigeria. Besides, the contractor was from this village. I can't remember his name and I don't want to, because I may snuff life out of him with my bare hands!

PAPA: (*Nodding.*) I was aware of his building construction along Kofo Abayomi Street. He showed me photographs of the project ...

JOHN-CAMPBELL: We saw those pictures, too ... they were scam, all lies!

PAPA: What about the man who handled the work? Didn't he refund the money to your father?

JOHN-CAMPBELL: No! Dad never heard anything from him again. The last time he came to Nigeria before he died, he chased this man from Lagos to Port Harcourt. Yet, he couldn't find him, not even his shadow. The man just disappeared. Dad was so angry. Mum, too! He returned to Chicago without coming here. We were broke. We sold our house because we could no longer pay the mortgage. We moved to a smaller house. Mum had to do two jobs. Then, they decided never again ... (*Gesturing with his hands.*) Never again to return to this country, not even for a visit, not to live ... Never!

PAPA: (*Surprised.*) Did things happen like this?

JOHN-CAMPBELL: Dad suddenly had a heart attack. Fortunately, it was a minor one. But he never felt well after these incidents.

PAPA: (*Looks up to the ceiling.*) Unfortunate! I was not aware that these things happened.

JOHN-CAMPBELL: When Mum and Dad died together in an accident, we decided to bury them there in Chicago. After all, they had decided not to return home again. But Dad's best friend who's from a neigbhouring village, advised us to take their bodies home as a form of announcement, too. He argued that doing so would serve as evidence for us and show eventually that we were truly from this village, because they would have been buried on their land and their tombs would have been engraved.

PAPA: (*Nods.*) Yes.

JOHN-CAMPBELL: We couldn't accompany their corpses even

though we had planned to. We had to deal with some problems that came up with our US passports. My sisters would have really loved to be here. They have never visited Nigeria. I hope they would someday though. That's if they find a reason to.

PAPA: Hmn! We hope … (*Amazed.*) At least, you have come to see me.

JOHN-CAMPBELL: Yeah … I am here. I've also come for something else, and it is very important. But we will talk about it after you've had your breakfast.

PAPA: Ok. The only food I have at home now is my evening meal which I failed to eat last night because I was too excited when you showed up. Your presence took my appetite away. But the food is there.

(*Pointing to the door.*)

Under the table in my room. We may just warm it and share. I'm very sure you never had *akpu* in America. We will eat it with bitter-leaf soup.

JOHN-CAMPBELL: Don't you worry, Grandpa. I brought you some bread and biscuits from Lagos. I even came with some Kellogg's cornflakes from the US. I'm sure you've never had this, too. You'll like it.

PAPA: Oh …

JOHN-CAMPBELL: Let me get you some bread first.

PAPA: Get on with it, my son.

JOHN-CAMPBELL: Do you want to have it with a cup of tea, coffee or just water?

PAPA: Whatever it is. I don't usually eat all these American foods. It may well be that my Christmas is here already. Let me join you and eat like the English queen.

JOHN-CAMPBELL: (*Laughing.*) You make me laugh, Grandpa.

I'd just get you a hot cup of coffee and some slices of bread. Where's the kitchen? I need to get us some hot water ...

PAPA: Behind the house. The brick hut close to the farm. I used the firewood last night so it won't take too long to burn.

JOHN-CAMPBELL: (*Surprised.*) You still cook, Grandpa?

PAPA: (*Confidently.*) Yes. I am too old to get another wife.

JOHN-CAMPBELL: (*Thoughtfully.*) That's not good. You'll kill yourself ...

PAPA: My neighbour's wife comes here often to help me cook soup. She makes them in her kitchen sometimes and even helps with the cultivation of the yams and cassava in the farm.

JOHN-CAMPBELL: (*Surprised.*) Hmn ... I am not surprised. That's one good thing you get here in Nigeria. You may never get this kind of help in the States. Who cares?

PAPA: Nigeria brings its own advantages.

JOHN-CAMPBELL: (*Standing up.*) I guess ... Let me get us breakfast.

PAPA: Please, go ahead.

JOHN-CAMPBELL: I'll be back with your food in a bit.

(*Exit* JOHN-CAMPBELL. PAPA *picks a newspaper that is on the chair, he opens it and starts flipping through the pages. After a minute,* JOHN-CAMPBELL *comes back onstage with a plastic tray – on it is a loaf of sliced bread placed on two rubber plates and two cups of coffee. He drops the tray on the centre table.*)

Here you go, Grandpa.

PAPA: Thank you, my son.

JOHN-CAMPBELL: (*Sits down.*) Thank you, too, Papa.

(*Looks around the house.*) You provided shelter.

PAPA: (*Laughing.*) And you have just provided food. We thank God.

(*Both* PAPA *and* JOHN-CAMPBELL *are quiet for a few seconds, then they start eating.* JOHN-CAMPBELL *moves his chair closer to the centre table. He takes one plate and places the other in front of* PAPA. PAPA *sips from his coffee while* JOHN-CAMPBELL *takes some slices of bread – he places some on* PAPA's *plate and some on his. They start eating.*)

You said something else brought you this far, besides wanting to see me.

JOHN-CAMPBELL: Yes, Papa. But we should eat first, I think.

PAPA: Go ahead, my son. What is it?

JOHN-CAMPBELL: Don't worry too much, Grandpa. Let us eat.

PAPA: We are eating ...

(*He drops his cup of coffee on the table and eats up the slice of bread in his right hand in a hurry.*)

Really, why have you come home?

JOHN-CAMPBELL: (*Sips from his coffee and drops the cup on the table.*) In fact, I returned two days ago from the United States with my fiancée. We plan to get married real soon. She remained in Lagos because we weren't sure of the accommodation here. She will join us soon anyway.

PAPA: (*Smiling.*) Marriage ... I am happy about that. You're a grown man, like your father.

JOHN-CAMPBELL: Yeah. We should have been married months ago. In short, we planned to get married five months ago in the States. But my wife has a very stubborn father. He is a professor of engineering at the university in Chicago. He insisted that I bring my people to his village to do the right thing. They are from Nwangwu-Akwu village. My wife said it's very close to ours.

PAPA: Yes ...

JOHN-CAMPBELL: Mandy describes her father's house all the time. She says it's a popular compound between the town's community bank and the village square, not far from their local deity.

PAPA: (*Thinking.*) Hmn ... What is her name? Mandy?

JOHN-CAMPBELL: Yeah. We call her Miss Mandy in the US. But she's Mandy. Just Mandy.

PAPA: (*Surprised.*) Is she not Igbo? Doesn't she have a native name? What is Mandy?

JOHN-CAMPBELL: (*Smiling.*) Yeah, Mandy is short for Chimamanda.

PAPA: (*Nodding slowly.*) Oh, I now see.

JOHN-CAMPBELL: Yes. Folks had to get used to Mandy because Chimamanda sounded like a tongue twister to the Americans. It was difficult for some of her teachers to pronounce. The name came from her teachers and friends in first grade. That's how it stuck.

PAPA: And her father's name is?

JOHN-CAMPBELL: Uzondu. But he's just known as Professor Phillip in the university campus and neigbourhood.

PAPA: (*Sighs.*) I know the family.

JOHN-CAMPBELL: (*Relieved.*) That's good, Papa, yeah.

PAPA: Hmn ... I don't know about good. Bluntly speaking, their grandfather's affair with that local deity was obviously wrong. That affair was neither blessed nor graced by society's blessings. I am not sure about good.

JOHN-CAMPBELL: (*Shocked.*) What do you mean, Papa? What blessings?

PAPA: Nwapa! That's the name your mother and father called you the day you were born.

(*There's a knock on the door. Shouts.*)

Who?

MADAM DO-GOOD: (*Answering from backstage.*) It's me, Papa.

JOHN-CAMPBELL: (*Cuts in; asking PAPA.*) Who?

PAPA: It is Madam Do-Good, my neighbour ... the kind woman who brings food to me sometimes and helps with the firewood.

(*Calling MADAM DO-GOOD.*) Come in, Do-Good.

She lives in the next compound where they sell 'em cocoyams.

JOHN-CAMPBELL: Oh, okay.

(*Enter MADAM DO-GOOD, a woman in her forties.*)

MADAM DO-GOOD: (*Coming in, genuflecting.*) Good morning, Papa.

PAPA: Eh heh, welcome, Do-Good.

JOHN-CAMPBELL: (*Greeting MADAM DO-GOOD.*) Good morning.

MADAM DO-GOOD: (*To JOHN-CAMPBELL.*) Morning, my son.

(*Addressing PAPA.*) I hope your sleep was peaceful, Papa.

PAPA: But for the mosquitoes, as usual, the night was more or less good. Good, meet my grandson, Nwapa, Chukwuemeka's first child and only son ...

JOHN-CAMPBELL: (*Standing up.*) Pleased to finally meet you.

(*He brings his right hand to shake MADAM DO-GOOD.*)

MADAM DO-GOOD: (*Coming closer to JOHN-CAMPBELL.*) I should hug you, my son.

(*Hugs JOHN-CAMPBELL for about five seconds.*)

I was at your parents' funeral.

(*With mixed feelings of joy and sadness.*)

Sad. (*Pitiful.*) Papa didn't take it well. It was sad for all of us.

JOHN-CAMPBELL: (*Calm.*) I feel you, neighbour. Aunty … I hope I can call you that. We were all shaken by my folks' sudden demise. But we're grown now, hopefully we'd continue in their shoes.

MADAM DO-GOOD: (*To* JOHN-CAMPBELL.) Amen, my son. As they say, it is well!

JOHN-CAMPBELL: (*Offering his seat to* MADAM DO-GOOD.) Please, sit, Madam.

MADAM DO-GOOD: (*To* JOHN-CAMPBELL.) No, thank you, Nwapa.

(*Addressing* PAPA.) I only came this morning to ask Papa what he'd want for his morning food.

(*Looking at the bread on the table.*) But I can see food here already.

PAPA: Do-Good! Thank you o, my daughter. Our good Lord will always reward you for your kindness. Your husband, too. Thank you.

JOHN-CAMPBELL: (*Sitting back down.*) Hmn …

MADAM DO-GOOD: Because I was planning to bring you some rice and plantain. I put the rice on fire before coming here.

PAPA: (*Grateful.*) God will do you good, my daughter.

MADAM DO-GOOD: Thank you, Papa. I will bring the food to you in the afternoon since you are eating already.

PAPA: (*Still grateful.*) Better.

MADAM DO-GOOD: (*To* JOHN-CAMPBELL.) I hope that my son wouldn't mind having hot rice and fried plantain for his meal, this afternoon.

JOHN-CAMPBELL: (*Smiles softly, grateful.*) I would like some, of course, Madam.

MADAM DO-GOOD: (*Eagerly.*) You will. I'm making kernel stew with some local herbs and some goat meat. I'm also frying the plantain with palm oil. You know it's rich in carotenoid and it lowers mortality from a number of chronic illnesses. (*Smiling.*) I know how cold it would have been for you in America. This soup would clear the cold immediately, all of it.

JOHN-CAMPBELL: (*Soft laughter.*) Thank you, Madam.

MADAM DO-GOOD: Fine, my dear. What should I have done? We are here for Papa and all his family. God placed us here to do to others what we would want them to do to us.

PAPA: (*Light laughter.*) You are a good woman, Do-Good. Our good Lord will guide you always. He will surely do you good!

JOHN-CAMPBELL: (*Nods in agreement.*) Indeed.

MADAM DO-GOOD: (*With calm.*) Let me go now and check my food. My husband may go to Nwangwu-Akwu today to buy some wood. He is making furniture for one banker who came in from Lagos. And, he has only three weeks to finish.

JOHN-CAMPBELL: (*To* PAPA.) That's Mandy's home.

MADAM DO-GOOD: (*To* JOHN-CAMPBELL.) Where?

PAPA: (*Sober.*) Don't worry there, Do-Good. Go to your kitchen before your food starts burning.

MADAM DO-GOOD: I will return in the afternoon then. (*Pointing at the bread on the table.*) I hope this holds your stomach till noon.

PAPA: It will.

MADAM DO-GOOD: (*To* PAPA *and* JOHN-CAMPBELL.) If not, I could come back with some rice before noon, so that you can have your afternoon meal earlier than usual.

PAPA: (*Grateful.*) This is strong enough, my daughter.

JOHN-CAMPBELL: (*To* MADAM DO-GOOD. *Also grateful.*) It is.

MADAM DO-GOOD: (*To* PAPA *and* JOHN-CAMPBELL.) If you say so. Let me run to my food.

(*To* JOHN-CAMPBELL.) Welcome, my son.

JOHN-CAMPBELL: (*Smiling.*) Thank you, Madam.

MADAM DO-GOOD: (*To* PAPA.) I will come back later.

PAPA: (*Thankful.*) You are too kind. Thank you. Please ask Ejike to pass through here on his way to the wood market. I may have a message I want him to take for me.

MADAM DO-GOOD: No problem, Papa.

(*Exit* MADAM DO-GOOD.)

PAPA: Hmn! (*Heaves a sigh of relief.*) Yes, we talked about the woman you are proposing to marry.

JOHN-CAMPBELL: Mandy, yes.

PAPA: (*Bluntly.*) Nwapa, going straight to the point ... Marrying anybody from Nwangwu-Akwu village is not a task for someone in your position.

JOHN-CAMPBELL: Yeah. Like I said, Mandy's father strongly insisted that we come down here to see my uncles so they would accompany me to her people to discuss and pay her bride price.

PAPA: (*Shaking his head in disagreement.*) You don't seem to understand me and I won't blame you. No one from the seven villages that make up our village group, goes to marry another, man or woman, from Nwangwu-Akwu. No freeborn who talks of marriage even steps foot in Nwangwu-Akwu.

JOHN-CAMPBELL: (*Shocked.*) Huh ... But Madam Do-Good just announced a few minutes ago that her husband will visit Nwangwu-Akwu, didn't she?

PAPA: (*Nodding in agreement.*) Yes. He's not going there to take a wife. It is because we are in the year 2014 that people like Ejike, Do-Good's husband, can walk into Nwangwu-Akwu village as a freeborn from this village to purchase any item, whether wood or garri. Sixty years ago, it was impossible. Even twenty years ago, no one dared!

JOHN-CAMPBELL: (*Still very shocked.*) So what? Are we cousins or some distant relatives? Is that what it is?

PAPA: My son.

JOHN-CAMPBELL: Papa.

PAPA: Marriage in this part of the world is not simple arithmetic. Too many factors, more than the couple involved, determine whether or not the marriage will happen.

JOHN-CAMPBELL: I don't understand. I've come all the way to West Africa just to please Mandy's traditional parents ... Now this ... Are we related to each other?

PAPA: (*Yawns.*) Nwapa, a chick that is close to the mother may enjoy a grasshopper thigh.

(*Clears throat.*) If one sees something wrong and says nothing about it, such wrong soon defeats him. Our people say that a man who follows the elephant, would never get entangled in the forest.

(*Clears throat.*) I know you haven't come this far to see me.

(JOHN-CAMPBELL *appears less concerned.*)

But, because you have come this far for the sake of marriage, I am sure your father and mother would have permitted me to explain the rules of our tradition, especially those regarding marriage, because this marriage would extend to every member of our family and those in Nwangwu-Akwu. And, if I pretend not to care about the traditional consequences of someone from this family marrying from Nwangwu-Akwu village ...

(*Pointing at the ground with his finger.*) No child from this family would forgive me. None!

JOHN-CAMPBELL: (*Wondering eagerly.*) So Mandy cannot be my wife?

PAPA: More than that ... You should not even be seen with her in this village. You may go to hers and be seen there with her. That may be safe for you. But here, you bring her with you, you cause the entire family's downfall.

JOHN-CAMPBELL: (*Surprised.*) What?

PAPA: (*Nodding.*) Our ruin; all of us ... Because I know our tradition is alien to you, I will tell you everything there is to know to convince your proposed wife and yourself that both of you would be better as friends, not married.

JOHN-CAMPBELL: (*Enthusiastic.*) Go on, Papa. Try and take my heart away from Mandy.

PAPA: Believe me, my son, it is not easy to talk about a belief in which one has no faith, at least in modern times. It is a hopeless situation, but one does not throw himself into such hopelessness because of love. Many things happened in the past, some, beyond our comprehension. We weren't born into any family or village group without traditions and culture. Our forebears had some traditions, which we still practise today, though in varying ramifications. Some seem to have disappeared; some are disappearing, while others refuse to leave us. Yet, I can say some changes have occurred in the last two decades, I believe. I never get tired of narrating the story of Nwakaego, whose husband was well known across several towns for his dealings with the colonial white men and their trade in tobacco, palm oil and slaves. He was the wealthiest black man everyone around here ever knew. But, he died before he was ripe. Nwakaego, his only wife, was threatened by her husband's brothers. They all craved his wealth, his barns, his colony of servants, even his dear wife. They didn't mourn him before they started fighting over everything he had. They all shared his belongings amongst themselves. Nwakaego wouldn't take any of this. Off she ran, to the sacred shrine of Amadioha.

(Immediately, the light on stage A becomes dim. After five seconds, bright lights come on stage B, revealing the Amadioha shrine. The shrine is carved in a small section of stage B. Some objects, like calabash and carved wooden items, can be seen inside the shrine, a semi-circled dwarf clay wall. A carved, black, wooden mask is seen at the centre of the shrine. White and red satin fabric can be seen tied around the shrine as earthen pots and leaves are scattered all around the stage. Some animal noises can be heard around the stage, indicating its location is in a forest. Enter NWAKAEGO, running in towards the shrine, worried, crying and looking around in fear. She's a woman in her late thirties. She is dressed in a traditional blouse and local wrapper. The same wrapper fabric is tied around her head. She kneels before the black wooden mask.)

NWAKAEGO: *(Still crying.)* God of my ancestors! God of my late husband, please, intercede for me. They have all come to reap where they did not sow. Nwefoke wants to eat the leftovers from his brother's plate of soup. How can I marry a drunk who doesn't know how to cut weed or cultivate yams? Amadioha, I have come to you. You are my only hope for survival, I can go no place else.

(Still crying, she picks up a knife from the floor of the shrine and lifts it up.) With this knife I offer myself to you, and as a form of sacrifice, I spill my blood here …

(She cuts her left thumb with the knife and spills the blood before the mask.) On your altar. And I declare, henceforth, that my family and I, everything I own, belong to you, great god of my forebears, today and forever. I take this oath in

expectation of your incessant guidance and protection over my family and I. We shall obey you at all times and worship you as long as we have breath in us. Amadioha, please, hear me!

(*She falls on her blood as light goes offstage. Bright light comes back on stage A.*)

JOHN-CAMPBELL: (*Fascinated.*) Is that so?

PAPA: (*Nodding.*) Yes. But do you blame Nwakaego? A rat does not run here and there in vain. Even the vulture, it does not circle without a reason, a good reason. She didn't have much choice. In fact, I wonder sometimes, what I would have done if I were in her shoes. Her in-laws came from nowhere to pounce on all her husband's labour. Yes, that used to be the tradition; it still is in some areas today. But the tradition was wicked in most cases. Women are ripped of their spouse's possessions, forced into marriage to his brother, whom they may not like, or sometimes thrown out of their family home. Nwakaego just had to protect her family. She ran off to Amadioha to achieve this.

JOHN-CAMPBELL: (*Still fascinated.*) How was Amadioha to protect them?

PAPA: The moment Nwakaego performed that sacrifice, everything she owned on earth, including her family, Nwakaego herself, their lives, belonged to Amadioha. And no one, not even the chief priest, dared to tamper in whatever form with the deity's possessions. That way, Nwakaego protected all her late husband's properties. Her in-laws ran very far from her and her children. Amadioha protected them all the time. They were safe from harm or embarrassments. But, this action had consequences. She, and all generations that would come from her children became *osu*. Slaves of the deity.

JOHN-CAMPBELL: (*Considering the message and shaking his head in disagreement.*) That's some very crude narration.

PAPA: Yes. (*Nodding in agreement.*) And in those days of our fathers, marriage to an *osu* was taboo and it was discouraged throughout the land. Associating with an *osu* was not commonplace and to even do so was to instantly join their fold. Many people joined this dreadful caste for different reasons and in many ways. But what was common then was by consecration a sacrifice to deities, just as Nwakaego did. Those who had twin children then, offered such children as sacrifices, too.

JOHN-CAMPBELL: (*Amazed.*) Even children?

PAPA: (*Nodding in agreement.*) Even children.

JOHN-CAMPBELL: (*Cutting in.*) I know that we had bad traditions in Africa before the British and their friends shared the continent. But I was not aware very heinous traditions such as these existed at that time. Maybe coming to Africa was the best thing our colonial masters did.

PAPA: (*Nodding in agreement.*) This didn't start as a form of wickedness or hatred for those concerned. It was the tradition of our forebears. In those days, to kill an animal that belonged to the deity was forbidden and the punishment of course was to replace the dead animal with a human sacrifice after some rituals had been performed. In most cases, the culprit was expected to offer a member of the family, who may be young or willing to take his place. If not, such culprit was to be the sacrifice. In some areas, where the culprit was a little child, such a child was immediately given as a replacement without much ado. Some villages also offered stubborn children, thieves and nuisances to deities to free their land of trouble. Like Nwakaego, who ran off to avoid harassment from her husband's people, criminals also took refuge in the shrines of very powerful deities to escape punishment of death. The worst thing anyone could do to them after their consecration was to insult them from a distance. That was all the power the freeborn had over them.

JOHN-CAMPBELL: (*Intrigued.*) Wow!

PAPA: (*Cutting in.*) That's not all. Some individuals and groups became members of the *osu* caste by other ways. A debtor spontaneously drove himself to servitude to dodge the payment of his debt or to escape harassments from his neighbours. The mere fact of crossing the innermost sanctuary of a deity's shrine even made one an *osu*. Hungry, frustrated people also surrendered themselves to deities, so they fed off gifts and sacrifices offered to their deities. They enjoyed all the goodies and domestic animals that their deities owned. They farmed on those lands that belonged to the deities, too. This is why some people argue that the *osu* population swelled in some areas.

JOHN-CAMPBELL: (*Cuts in.*) What's the connection to my fiancée?

PAPA: Nwakaego's generation are the present inhabitants of Nwangwu-Akwu. The woman you call your fiancée, belongs to the generation Nwakaego offered to Amadioha several decades ago.

JOHN-CAMPBELL: (*Cuts in.*) You're not sure, Papa.

PAPA: But ...

JOHN-CAMPBELL: (*Cuts in.*) Even so, I don't see why I can't marry Mandy. All these happened in the past. We've all had good and bad experiences in the past, but we must move on from them and become better people. My father always told us that the lion's power lies in our fear of it and I am not afraid to make a move no one has before.

PAPA: Your father was not wrong. I trained him. However, this is a different subject and we didn't make such tradition.

JOHN-CAMPBELL: (*Cuts in.*) But you're part of it now, if not, what's the reason for narrating these tales of sacrifices since they no longer happen?

(*There's a knock on the door.*)

PAPA: Who?

EJIKE: (*From backstage.*) It's me, Ejikeojiaku!

PAPA: (*Stands up.*) Please, come in, Ejike.

(*Enter* EJIKE, *a man in his late forties. He is wearing a long-sleeved shirt and a pair of jump-up trousers. The sleeves of his shirt are unbuttoned. He walks in roughly with a sack of tools in his right hand and a pencil on his right ear.* PAPA *stops him close to the door as he prevents him from getting close to* JOHN-CAMPBELL.)

EJIKE: Good morning, Papa.

PAPA: Welcome, Ejike.

EJIKE: Is that emmm ... ?

PAPA: Nwapa!

EJIKE: Yes! Do-Good told me that he arrived yesterday.

PAPA: Yes, he did.

EJIKE: (*To* JOHN-CAMPBELL.) Welcome, young man. How is *obodo oyibo*?

JOHN-CAMPBELL: (*Smiling softly.*) We are fine. Thank you, Sir. Welcome, too.

PAPA: (*Whispering.*) Do-Good was ...

EJIKE: (*Cuts in.*) Yes. She told me that you wanted to give me a message before I left for the market.

PAPA: (*Whispering.*) Yes. Please, I don't want my son to hear us.

EJIKE: (*Nods as he whispers.*) That's fine, Papa.

PAPA: (*Whispering.*) She told me you were going to Nwangwu-Akwu today.

EJIKE: (*Cuts in, still whispering.*) Yes, to buy some wood and other materials ...

PAPA: (*Whispering.*) Please, I want you to find out more about this Professor Uzondu and his family. They say his house is by the village square.

EJIKE: (*Nods as he whispers.*) Oh, the one in America?

PAPA: (*Whispering.*) Yes, Ejike. My friend's son wants to take a wife from his household.

EJIKE: (*Nods as he whispers.*) This means you want me to find out if the coast is clear?

PAPA: (*Nods.*) Exactly.

EJIKE: (*Whispering.*) We all know what they are ...

PAPA: (*Whispering.*) Yes. But I'd like us to be very sure. The family involved here is too close to me. I cannot give them some information which I haven't verified. Just in case I am wrong.

EJIKE: (*Still whispering.*) True. Marriage is too serious to just dwell on rumours.

PAPA: (*Nods.*) Certainly.

EJIKE: (*Nodding in agreement.*) Then I will go there, Papa.

PAPA: (*Grateful.*) Eh heh, go well, Ejike.

EJIKE: (*To* NWAPA.) Bye-bye, our son from the white man's land.

(*Smiles flagrantly. Exit* EJIKE.)

PAPA: (*Walking back to his seat.*) That was Madam Do-Good's husband.

JOHN-CAMPBELL: I thought so.

PAPA: (*Sits down.*) I gave him a message for my friend who

lives along the road to his timber market. I hope he delivers the message early enough. My son ...

JOHN-CAMPBELL: Papa.

PAPA: Certain things, we can't change. But we must try not to break existing customs and live with what is until these things die naturally.

JOHN-CAMPBELL: Things cannot change when those who should change them continue to make them stay. Obviously, you have made it clear that you do not approve of my marriage to Mandy.

PAPA: (*Nodding his head slowly.*) I haven't said anything like that. It is too early for me to approve or disapprove of your marriage to this strange girl.

JOHN-CAMPBEL: (*Surprised.*) Strange girl? What's strange about her? I practically live with her in the US.

PAPA: (*Surprised.*) Nwapa, marriage is not straightforward anywhere in the world. Here, marriage goes beyond a man and his wife. It also involves close kin.

JOHN-CAMPBELL: Yes, that is why I have come home with my wife to see you and her family.

PAPA: It involves more than seeing me or the girl's father. Before a young man starts talking about marriage, he must first speak to his parents just like you're doing now. Your parents would now approve or disapprove. But before they take a decision, if the girl or her family is unknown to them, they must send emissaries to visit the girl's village to do a little investigation on her family background.

JOHN-CAMPBELL: And ...

PAPA: Checking her background usually takes a day or more, depending on the distance and other issues that may arise. The reason for this is to know if the girl or her parents have suspicious backgrounds or are social outcasts. In the meantime, before we disperse emissaries to the girl's village, we must watch her first, that is, if we've met her. This is usually the first hurdle, and the second stage of going into family background is only done where this is successful. On the other side, the girl's family also carries out similar investigations on their would-be son-in-law and his family. Both bride and bridegroom are usually unaware of these checks as they are done quietly. Before now, you, the young man, should have visited the father of the girl in the company of your father and a few male figures in our extended family to ask for the bride's hand in marriage. It is this act that now prompts the bride's parents to conduct their investigation. Where there is a problem, like in this case where the girl involved is *osu*, it is my duty to tell you that no road leads to that place and that you must look elsewhere for marriage.

JOHN-CAMPBELL: (*Shaking his head slowly in disagreement.*) This is a big joke.

PAPA: (*Cuts in.*) It is only when these enquiries on both sides are complete that both families work towards settling the bride price. This must, of course, include the members of our extended family. And we cannot do otherwise.

JOHN-CAMPBELL: (*Surprised.*) Even in this day and age?

PAPA: (*Nodding his head in agreement.*) Even in this day and age.

JOHN-CAMPBELL: (*Resisting.*) No. I'm not an imbecile. I will not sit here while a group of old men, village people, decide whether or not I marry a woman I have longed to spend the rest of my life with. (*His phone beeps in his breast pocket. He brings it out to read a text he just received.*) In short, the text that just came into my phone was from Mandy. She's leaving Lagos now. She'd arrive here in the afternoon.

PAPA: (*Surprised.*) Oh! She's on her way already ...

JOHN-CAMPBELL: Yes, Papa.

PAPA: (*Shaking his head slowly*.) And where's she going, her father's house?

JOHN-CAMPBELL: Maybe here, maybe there. I'm not sure. It'll depend on when she gets to Onitsha. She's travelling by road and from what I've seen, the roads are bad enough to keep them for a long time. If she's too tired when she gets to Onitsha, she'd simply come here to spend the night.

PAPA: (*Uninterested*.) Hmm.

   (*Lights fade slowly.*)

Scene Two

Lights come on stage A, revealing JOHN-CAMPBELL in PAPA's parlour, just as in Scene One. JOHN-CAMPBELL sits comfortably on a chair in the room as he talks to MANDY on his mobile phone. MANDY's voice can be heard lightly on the stage.

JOHN-CAMPBELL: (*Excitedly.*) You guys must be close to Onitsha now.

MANDY: Do I know where that is?

JOHN-CAMPBELL: You should ask someone in your coach so that they don't take you to another bus stop.

MANDY: Don't worry, I'm focused on the signs.

JOHN-CAMPBELL: Well, it won't hurt to just ask.

MANDY: Don't worry about me, John. I'll be there sooner than you expect.

JOHN-CAMPBELL: Just be safe.

MANDY: I am. How is it going down there? How is your grandfather? Does he know now?

JOHN-CAMPBELL: Yes, he does.

MANDY: (*Sounding excited.*) So?

JOHN-CAMPBELL: So, yes, I told him.

MANDY: (*Sounding a bit disappointed.*) I know you told him. What did he say?

JOHN-CAMPBELL: Were you expecting him to say something?

MANDY: John, what's the matter with you? Why are you overlooking my concerns?

JOHN-CAMPBELL: Your concerns? How?

MANDY: I thought the reason we've come down to Nigeria is for your people to meet mine? Is that not what you discussed with your grandfather?

JOHN-CAMPBELL: Yes. And I've just informed you that I told him. Were you expecting him to say yes or no?

MANDY: (*Angrily.*) Don't worry about what I was expecting or not. I will see you when I get there. Bye.

JOHN-CAMPBELL: (*Unconcerned.*) Oh, bye! (*Immediately puts the phone in his breast pocket.*) I'm not sure what has gotten to Mandy's head.

(*There's a knock on the door.*)

Who is it, please?

(*Enter* MADAM DO-GOOD, *carrying two food flasks in a plastic basket.*)

MADAM DO-GOOD: It is me, Nwapa.

JOHN-CAMPBELL: (*Standing up to help* MADAM DO-GOOD *carry the basket.*) Oh, welcome, Madam.

MADAM DO-GOOD: Don't worry about it. It is not heavy at all. How are you?

JOHN-CAMPBELL: I am fine, thanks.

MADAM DO-GOOD: (*Drops basket on the centre table.*) What about Papa? Did he go out?

JOHN-CAMPBELL: No. He's inside, sleeping.

MADAM DO-GOOD: Okay. I brought your food as I promised.

JOHN-CAMPBELL: (*Happy.*) Thank you very much, Madam. Thank you.

MADAM DO-GOOD: Don't thank me too much, Nwapa. I have gotten so used to preparing meals for your grandfather. You know I was his nurse for some time.

JOHN-CAMPBELL: (*Surprised.*) You're a nurse?

MADAM DO-GOOD: A qualified one, with a university degree.

JOHN-CAMPBELL: No wonder you know about the carotenoid in palm oil.

MADAM DO-GOOD: (*Both of them smile together.*) Yes. I had to stop practising for a while because I moved with my husband to the village.

JOHN-CAMPBELL: (*Interested.*) Yeah, I noticed that a lot of African women suspend their careers for their husbands.

MADAM DO-GOOD: (*Nodding approval.*) What can we do? The man heads the family.

JOHN-CAMPBELL: (*Showing his disapproval.*) It's not a good thing to do. You see, you can also contribute financially to your family when you work. Two hands will feed the family better than one.

MADAM DO-GOOD: Yes. But I've not stopped working. I assist people here when they have problems that require little medical attention … Just like I do for your grandfather.

JOHN-CAMPBELL: And you have the licence to do that?

MADAM DO-GOOD: Yes. I told you that I have a bachelor's degree in nursing.

JOHN-CAMPBELL: (*Remembering.*) Then you would do very well in the US. We have many Nigerian nurses there. And they do very well in their chosen profession.

MADAM DO-GOOD: Yes. Some of my colleagues ran there for greener pastures. I hear from them sometimes.

JOHN-CAMPBELL: That's good. Let me tell Papa that you're here.

MADAM DO-GOOD: (*In a low tone, directing him with her right hand.*) No, don't bother, Nwapa. Let us sit down for a moment to talk, please.

JOHN-CAMPBELL: Okay, Madam. (*They both sit.*)

MADAM DO-GOOD: You see, I don't want to put my mouth in

matters that do not concern me. But I am concerned now, that is why I want to ask … did you come home to take a wife? Because I know some very good girls around.

JOHN-CAMPBELL: (*Smiling.*) Yes, but I came with a girl from the United States.

MADAM DO-GOOD: (*Surprised.*) Oh.

JOHN-CAMPBELL: She's from Nwangwu-Akwu village.

MADAM DO-GOOD: (*Surprised.*) Ah, that's where my husband goes to buy materials.

JOHN-CAMPBELL: Papa told me.

MADAM DO-GOOD: (*In a lower tone.*) Where is she?

JOHN-CAMPBELL: She will be here today.

MADAM DO-GOOD: And Papa knows that this woman you intend to marry is from Nwangwu-Akwu?

JOHN-CAMPBELL: He does.

MADAM DO-GOOD: He hasn't told you anything, has he?

JOHN-CAMPBELL: He did, in fact.

MADAM DO-GOOD: (*Curious.*) What did he say?

JOHN-CAMPBELL: He talked about Nwangwu-Akwu people belonging to some fetish deity …

MADAM DO-GOOD: Hmm, he told you the truth.

JOHN-CAMPBELL: Come on, Madam, why do you people choose to live with some old customs? The world has obviously gone beyond this.

MADAM DO-GOOD: I don't disagree, Nwapa.

JOHN-CAMPBELL: So, why do we have to keep talking about who is *osu* or not?

MADAM DO-GOOD: This *osu* caste issue is a very sensitive subject to discuss anywhere in Igboland. People don't usually call the word *osu* without turning to know who and who is around. Is Papa saying that you shouldn't marry the girl?

JOHN-CAMPBELL: He hasn't come out straight to say that. But I can sense his objection from his body language. Mandy is *osu*, tainted by association, as if to burn his words permanently into my head. I have never heard anything about this tradition before in my life. But I understand that what Papa was trying to say to me in a colourful way was that my Mandy is contaminated, like germs on good food or like food that has fallen to the dogs. How can Papa just say (*mimicking* PAPA) you won't marry Mandy, she is *osu*? He doesn't even know her.

MADAM DO-GOOD: But you know that Papa is an old man. He will not tell you anything that he doesn't want you to hear. He will come from his angle alone. You will be amazed at the things we do in this part of the world. Anyway, I will advise you to keep pushing. No one in this village is strong enough to decide who you should marry. The *osu* practice was abolished by a bill of the old East Regional House of Assembly in 1956. After that abolition, several villages, including ours and that of your wife, abolished the practice in their communities. So, I won't bother too much about your grandfather and his people. Yes, they will oppose and oppose, eventually, they will allow you to marry your heart-throb. But you must persist and show them that you are serious.

JOHN-CAMPBELL: (*Happy.*) Thank you, Madam. At least, someone in this village is on my side. I will insist on Mandy, don't worry.

MADAM DO-GOOD: It won't be very easy. Papa and your father's people will push you to the wall.

JOHN-CAMPBELL: Don't worry about that one.

MADAM DO-GOOD: Okay. I have to leave soon. My husband may return soon.

JOHN-CAMPBELL: (*Digging his right hand into his breast pocket.*) That's fine, Madam.

(*Handing* MADAM DO-GOOD *a fifty dollar bill he removed from his breast pocket.*) Thank you very much for your kind words.

MADAM DO-GOOD: (*Excitedly looking at the dollar bill.*) No, Nwapa. I should be thanking you. God will bless you.

JOHN-CAMPBELL: (*Nods.*) Amen.

MADAM DO-GOOD: You will marry the lady you want to marry.

JOHN-CAMPBELL: (*Nods.*) Amen.

MADAM DO-GOOD: (*Standing up,* JOHN-CAMPBELL *gets up too.*) Please, greet Papa very well for me. I am sure you people will enjoy the food. I will return later for my basket, please.

JOHN-CAMPBELL: No problem, Madam. I'll just go in now to give Papa his food. Thank you.

MADAM DO-GOOD: Okay. (*Exit.*)

JOHN-CAMPBELL: (*Sitting back, taking his mobile phone from his breast pocket.*) Mandy hasn't called to say where she is …

(*Looks at his wristwatch, he dials her number and puts the phone to his ear.*)

Hello, where are you now?

MANDY: (*Her voice can be heard slightly.*) We are heading to Asaba now.

JOHN-CAMPBELL: Okay. I was worried. You didn't call for some time.

MANDY: You didn't know that you upset me?

JOHN-CAMPBELL: I'm sorry, my love. You know how stressful this trip has been for us.

MANDY: (*Sounding concerned.*) Don't worry, John. We'll be back to the US in a few days. All this will be over soon.

JOHN-CAMPBELL: Okay. Just get here soon.

MANDY: We just got to Asaba. I can see the Niger Bridge from here.

JOHN-CAMPBELL: You'll soon arrive Onitsha then.

MANDY: I guess.

JOHN-CAMPBELL: Okay. Have a safe trip. I'll see you soon.

MANDY: Bye.

(*Enter* PAPA.)

JOHN-CAMPBELL: You're up already, Papa.

PAPA: Yes. Who was that on the phone?

JOHN-CAMPBELL: (*Puts phone back in his breast pocket.*) Mandy. She's very close to Onitsha now.

PAPA: I hope you are considering what we discussed earlier.

JOHN-CAMPBELL: I am, Papa.

PAPA: Okay. (*Goes to sit down, he sees* MADAM DO-GOOD's *basket on the table.*) Do-Good came?

JOHN-CAMPBELL: Yes. She left a few minutes ago.

PAPA: Okay.

JOHN-CAMPBELL: Madam Do-Good told me a lot about the caste tradition. She says it's been abolished many times.

PAPA: (*Insincere smile.*) She told you that. And then?

JOHN-CAMPBELL: We didn't have to go through all the stories about Mandy's family belonging to local gods.

PAPA: Most of those abolition attempts Do-Good told you about were shams to deceive the *osu* people into believing that their problems were over. It didn't take the practice away. I was there in 1975, when a neigbouring village displayed this kind of sham. Too many dignitaries attended the ceremony, including the Minister of Information, Culture and Tourism. The event was even broadcast live on TV. When the time came for the highest chief in the town, a ninety-year-old man who was the custodian of culture and traditions in the village, to perform the rituals of abolition, the old man stood at the centre of the congregation and was given seven kola nuts to pray and break and declare the practice abolished in the town. As the old man fumbled with one of the kola nuts, he became the target of a battery of eyes. What the people didn't know was that the old man was wiser than all of them who came together. He used a language with which he circumvented, cornered the whole functions and nobody understood it until afterwards. I will not tell you what the old man said, but he did this to avoid attracting the wrath of the deities to his head. Yet, the *osu* system continues to be practised in this village and other villages that attempted to abolish it. Most villages continue to hold abolition ceremonies every year. But, no traditional ruler in Igboland has sincerely abolished the practice. None! So, forget what Do-Good has said. Beautiful words don't necessarily express true sentiments. The leprosy says it loves you while it is eating your fingers.

(*Lights fade.*)

Scene Three

Darkness. There's a knock on the door. Lights come on stage A. PAPA's parlour. Enter PAPA, moving straight to the exit door.

PAPA: Who?

EJIKE: Ejike.

PAPA: (*Opening the door.*) You are back.

    (*Enter EJIKE.*)

EJIKE: Yes, Papa.

PAPA: What did you hear?

EJIKE: The family is not good. They are *osu*. I spoke to a few people, some elderly, even neighbours of the Uzondu's and they told me that the children from that lineage are very intelligent. They have the most professors from any family in that village.

PAPA: Don't worry about those details, Ejike.

EJIKE: (*Concerned.*) Who's the family interested in marrying from the professor's household?

PAPA: My grandson.

EJIKE: (*Shocked.*) *Tufiakwa*! Why? He doesn't know any other girl outside that family?

PAPA: (*Quietly.*) I don't know.

EJIKE: Papa, your boy is very handsome o. All the girls in this village will kill themselves to stand beside him forever. Please, talk to him to reconsider. He doesn't know she is *osu* and we cannot marry them?

PAPA: I talked to him this morning. Do-Good also spoke to him.

EJIKE: (*Nodding approval.*) That is good.

PAPA: But I get the feeling that she encouraged him to marry the *osu* girl.

EJIKE: (*Uncomprehendingly.*) No, Papa. She cannot do that.

PAPA: She did.

EJIKE: (*In disbelief.*) How? (*Angry.*) Let me go, Papa. I will see you later. (*Exit.*)

PAPA: Okay.

(*Lights fade.*)

Scene Four

Lights come on stage A, still in PAPA's parlour, just as in Scene One. JOHN-CAMPBELL is seen on PAPA's three-seater armchair, lying in a weary manner. He has an open book – a Nigerian novel – lying on his chest. He is sleeping and snoring heavily. There is a sudden knock on the door. JOHN-CAMPBELL is still snoring. A mobile phone in his breast pocket starts ringing. He jumps up immediately. The novel falls to the ground.

JOHN-CAMPBELL: (*Removing his phone from his breast pocket and receiving his call.*) Hello, sweetie … Sorry, I was sleeping. Where are you now? (*He takes the novel from the floor and places it on the chair.*)

MANDY: (*Speaking to JOHN-CAMPBELL on the phone. Her voice can be heard backstage.*) I'm right in front of your grandfather's house. Have you gone out?

JOHN-CAMPBELL: (*Surprised.*) No, no, no … I'm right here. Wait a minute, let me get the door. (*He puts his phone back in his pocket as he moves to open the door.*)

(*Enter MANDY, a beautiful lady of about twenty-five years. She is wearing heavy make-up with fixed eyelashes, dark eyebrows, pink lips and blush on her cheeks. She also wears a long black wig, which flows right in front of her, by the left side of her face and a long colourful satin gown that flows right to the ground. She walks in rolling a pink plastic box behind her. She speaks with a strong accent, too.*)

MANDY: (*Tired.*) I've been knocking … Didn't you hear me knock?

JOHN-CAMPBELL: (*Shutting the door.*) I'm so sorry. I was very tired. I was sleeping. (*Moves to hug MANDY.*) You don't even care to give me a hug?

MANDY: (*Uninterested.*) I'm so tired, John.

JOHN-CAMPBELL: I know.

MANDY: The roads are so bad. I'd have come by air.

JOHN-CAMPBELL: That would have been a better option if we had an airport around.

MANDY: I don't believe how backward things are around here. Even getting a ticket at the bus park was so difficult. Touts hang on everywhere. They charged me for everything.

JOHN-CAMPBELL: Because they know that you're a visitor …

MANDY: Is it that obvious?

JOHN-CAMPBELL: Please, sit. (*They both sit on the three-seater armchair.*)

MANDY: (*Looking around.*) Where is your grandfather? Is he sleeping, too?

JOHN-CAMPBELL: (*Looks towards the door.*) I don't even know. I was here alone.

MANDY: Oh, I see.

(*Looking at* JOHN-CAMPBELL *sympathetically.*) You look very thin already.

(*She feels his left cheek with her right palm.*) I hope you've had something good to eat since you got here.

JOHN-CAMPBELL: Yes, of course. My grandfather feeds very well here.

MANDY: (*Surprised.*) Oh, he cooks?

JOHN-CAMPBELL: Yes. Plus, he gets a lot of help from a good woman. She's a neighbour who lives by the fence. She knew my parents.

MANDY: Okay.

JOHN-CAMPBELL: How was your trip?

MANDY: (*Apathetic.*) Please … I don't want to talk about it. You know, it is shocking to see how bad things are in this country. The politicians here have properties in Dubai, United Kingdom, Indonesia, United States and all. They travel around the world in so much comfort. They see all the good things abroad. The good roads, the good hospitals and schools … real development. Yet, they get back home and find it difficult to replicate what their eyes have seen in these countries? I find it difficult to comprehend.

JOHN-CAMPBELL: (*Agreeing.*) It's the same talk everywhere. No one understands how things work here. It's funny, you know. A man occupies an office for a number of years and he fails to do the things expected of him, at least, fulfil the promises he made when he campaigned to occupy such office. What's the difficulty in providing basic amenities such as clean water, good roads, housing? Even good education and a proper health care system … These things are not very difficult to provide and, of course, we have all the resources to make them available to the common man. This is why I choose not to talk about this country because we rant and rant, yet, these men do whatever they like, with impunity.

MANDY: Imagine what happens when they leave office. They end up using or not using what they provided and what they haven't. Of course, they can't keep flying their private jets around and drinking bottled water. They must ply these bad roads, too. So what is the problem?

JOHN-CAMPBELL: It's simply because they spend most of their time abroad holidaying on beaches and yachts in Barbados and Morocco. They don't care about the middle-class and those who can't reach this class. Whenever they are in Nigeria they only lounge in their homes in Abuja, Lagos or Port Harcourt. But life is a circle, this is why I don't worry too much. These things will come back to hunt them. We always reap what we sow.

MANDY: I think so, too.

JOHN-CAMPBELL: I hate to talk about the drama in this country, please …

MANDY: Yeah. I hope we can do what we've come for and go back home. I'm already sick and tired of the weather. It's so hot and dry.

JOHN-CAMPBELL: It's because of the period we've come in. I hope we can leave soon though.

PAPA: (*Calling from backstage.*) Nwapa.

MANDY: (*A bit startled.*) Who's that? Is that your grandfather?

JOHN-CAMPBELL: (*To* MANDY.) Yes.

MANDY: What is he calling you?

JOHN-CAMPBELL: (*To* PAPA.) I am out here, Grandpa.

(*Enter* PAPA, *he stands close to the door and remains there. Immediately,* MANDY *gets up to greet him.*)

MANDY: (*Genuflecting lightly.*) Good afternoon, Papa.

PAPA: (*Not very friendly.*) Good evening, young lady. Did you just get here?

MANDY: Well, not too long ago.

JOHN-CAMPBELL: She came in about ten minutes ago. We didn't want to disturb you when she arrived.

PAPA: (*To* MANDY.) How was your journey?

MANDY: It was rough. But I'm here now.

PAPA: Oh, we give God the glory.

JOHN-CAMPBELL: Yes.

PAPA: I hope you didn't find it difficult to locate our house.

MANDY: No, it was easy. Immediately I called the name, someone led me straight to this house … a very kind man.

PAPA: Yes, most people in this village know their way to this compound. You're welcome.

MANDY: Thank you, Papa.

PAPA: Please, sit.

MANDY: (*Genuflects humbly*.) Thank you.

PAPA: Nwapa, please, make sure she gets something to eat before she leaves.

JOHN-CAMPBELL: (*Uncertain*.) Hmmn, okay, Grandpa.

PAPA: I am in my room.

JOHN-CAMPBELL: Okay.

(*Exit* PAPA.)

MANDY: Why does he keep calling you Nwapa? Is that the Igbo translation of John?

JOHN-CAMPBELL: (*Smiling lightly*.) No. It's my Igbo name. That's what he's used to. I don't blame him. John-Campbell is too foreign for his tongue.

MANDY: Okay. So where am I going to sleep? Your grandfather sounded like I wasn't welcome to sleep here.

JOHN-CAMPBELL: No. He may have been joking because I think it's already too late to go in search of a good hotel.

MANDY: I thought so, too.

JOHN-CAMPBELL: Yes.

MANDY: Have you told him why we made this trip?

JOHN-CAMPBELL: Yes, indeed. That's why he was expecting you.

MANDY: What do we have to do now? I really want us to get over with this stage of our marriage so that we can move on to the next stage in the US. That's the bit that I'm willing to stress myself for. I'm only doing this aspect because my folks insist. If not, I do not think that it is necessary.

JOHN-CAMPBELL: I think that we will be safer fulfilling all rites of marriage so that people won't come from anywhere to say that we haven't done things the right way. You know how these people could be. It would only cause us stress, which would be for a little while.

MANDY: It's alright. We are doing it already.

JOHN-CAMPBELL: Let me take you inside so that you can take a nap.

MANDY: Exactly what I need now.

(*They get up together*).

JOHN-CAMPBELL: I'll take your bag. (*Takes MANDY's luggage.*)

MANDY: Thanks.

(*Exeunt. Enter JOHN-CAMPBELL after thirty seconds. He sits at one end of the sitting room, takes his book, opens it and starts reading. Then enter PAPA, tying a local fabric over his white singlet. He comes along with a newspaper, sits at another end of the room and starts looking through the pages of the newspaper. JOHN-CAMPBELL looks at PAPA, ignores him and continues reading his book. Both men behave like they are not on talking terms. Enter EJIKE and MADAM DO-GOOD. PAPA is still reading his newspaper seriously.*)

EJIKE: (*Looks at MADAM DO-GOOD, then PAPA.*) Good afternoon, Papa.

PAPA: (*Looking at EJIKE and MADAM DO-GOOD.*) You're here already, Ejike ... and Do-Good ... Welcome. Please, come and sit.

JOHN-CAMPBELL: (*To MADAM DO-GOOD.*) Welcome, Madam.

EJIKE: (*Moving to sit, he sits close to JOHN-CAMPBELL, MADAM DO-GOOD and PAPA.*) Thank you, Papa.

(*To* JOHN-CAMPBELL.) How are you, Nwapa?

JOHN-CAMPBELL: (*Grins.*) I am fine, Sir. Welcome.

EJIKE: Okay. You're welcome, too. (*To* PAPA.) Well, Papa, I've come with my wife to see you and apologise for the discussions she had with Nwapa.

(JOHN-CAMPBELL *is surprised, but listens quietly. He closes his novel and drops it on the chair.*)

What she did this afternoon was not proper and I promise you that her intentions were never to cause problems in your family, between you and your grandson.

PAPA: (*Clears his throat.*) I know, Ejike.

EJIKE: (*To* JOHN-CAMPBELL.) My brother, Nwapa, the way we do things is different from the way you people do it in America.

JOHN-CAMPBELL: (*Courteously.*) Okay.

EJIKE: Papa told me that you want to marry a girl. My wife discussed it with me, too. The road to this family you want to marry from is not straight. Papa must have mentioned this to you. You cannot marry her if you want to save your family all the trouble. Papa is old, we don't want to cause him any headache. You think I didn't meet beautiful ladies that I could marry? In short, I had one who also had very wealthy parents. Her parents were willing to buy me a house, cars and even send me abroad. Yet, I couldn't marry her. To do that was to break my family's heart. I have a Higher National Diploma, but I'm here in this village doing woodwork. Marriage should not always be about riches or even love. Yes, it shouldn't be just convenient for you and the girl alone, but for your entire family. You must reason with your grandfather, please. You cannot marry an *osu*.

JOHN-CAMPBELL: (*Resisting.*) She wasn't born *osu*. Her family has been free from that horrid tag all their life and she has been away from Nigeria almost all her life. Uncle, all of you know nothing of her struggles, nothing of her strength and perseverance and absolutely nothing about her love for me. Yet, you ask me not to marry Mandy.

PAPA: (*To* JOHN-CAMPBELL.) You cannot spoil the family history and lineage by tainting it with *osu* blood. Once you do a thing like that, you stand alone and against members of your kindred.

JOHN-CAMPBELL: Papa, I am not interested in tainting anybody's history or lineage. I thought we were talking about my life here? Why do we keep talking about the extended family?

(*Enter* MANDY *suddenly. The stage is quiet for some seconds.* PAPA, EJIKE *and* MADAM DO-GOOD *look away and avoid body contact with* MANDY.)

MANDY: (*To everyone.*) Good afternoon. (*There's no response from anyone.*)

JOHN-CAMPBELL: (*Gesturing with his right hand.*) Boo-boo, please, come and sit.

MANDY: (*Moves closer to* JOHN-CAMPBELL *to sit.* PAPA *gets up and exits stage. After five seconds,* EJIKE *and* MADAM DO-GOOD *exit from the main exit.*) What is happening, John? What did I do? Why did they just ignore me?

JOHN-CAMPBELL: Mandy, please, ignore these people. They will come off this soon.

MANDY: (*Not happy.*) What's the problem? Is it because I am sleeping here tonight?

JOHN-CAMPBELL: No. Just ignore them, please.

MANDY: (*Angry.*) Look, John, you're beginning to get on my nerves. You better tell me what is happening now. I thought we vowed not to keep secrets?

JOHN-CAMPBELL: If you insist. They were expressing their concerns about some archaic traditions of your village people.

MANDY: The caste thing?

JOHN-CAMPBELL: Yes. (*Surprised.*) How come?

MANDY: My father told me that this may come up. But he said that it wouldn't cause anyone headache.

JOHN-CAMPBELL: So?

MANDY: So what?

JOHN-CAMPBELL: Your people are *osu*?

MANDY: Look, John, I do not want us to get into any argument because of something my forebears were involved in.

JOHN-CAMPBELL: We haven't entered into an argument yet.

MANDY: So …

JOHN-CAMPBELL: I think this is something we must talk about.

MANDY: Yes …

JOHN-CAMPBELL: We can't just ignore it. These people in this village know far more about tradition than all of us who reside in the United States and somehow, I think we'll be doing ourselves much good to listen and hear them out.

MANDY: What did they tell you? What have you heard?

JOHN-CAMPBELL: Grandpa told me that everyone in your village may be *osu*, at least, the majority.

MANDY: And if they are?

JOHN-CAMPBELL: This means you are one of them.

MANDY: And you have a problem with it?

JOHN-CAMPBELL: It's not like I do, but …

MANDY: You know everything about me. You know where I have been. You know where I was born and where I lived all my life. You've known me for a long time … yet, this village or group you talk about, you want to place me in it?

JOHN-CAMPBELL: I haven't done that yet, Mandy.

MANDY: What then are you doing?

JOHN-CAMPBELL: I am trying to understand your status. Please, do not make this difficult for me.

MANDY: How difficult would it get for you? It's me who gets all the name calling for something I know nothing about.

JOHN-CAMPBELL: I haven't called you names, my dear Mandy.

MANDY: (*Sober.*) Few years ago, when I attended the Igbo congress meeting in the States with Aunty Nkiru, a group of people came out from nowhere and started calling me and my sisters outcasts. I wasn't sure what they talked about, so I did the natural thing and ignored them. It was when I went to the ladies to take a pee that I eavesdropped on their conversation. One of them told her friends that her parents asked her to stay away from me and my sisters, that we were messengers of the gods. You know how funny that sounds? I laughed and laughed and wondered what god they spoke about. It was not until I got home and narrated the story to my folks that they started telling me how our forefathers became slaves to the local deity and how they and their descendants became tabooed. There and then they assured me that the past had nothing to do with us because the tradition had since been abolished. So I'm here now, wondering what you are talking about.

JOHN-CAMPBELL: I had the same thoughts when Grandpa narrated the story of the outcasts to me. Like you, I told him that it was a past that had no connection with your present generation. He, however, told me that once one is born into such family, the stigma remains with him and that nothing can take such stigma away, unless death.

MANDY: And that affects our marriage?

JOHN-CAMPBELL: You know me; I had a different view on issues like this before now. Grandpa has made things clearer a bit. I now understand the consequences of doing things like this without hearing from those who were here before us. My father always says that a man who urinates in a stream should always remember that his family would drink the same water. I am not in a hurry to act on the new information we have now about this practice. But I want us to do everything necessary to make sure that we do not take any decision that would cause problems for our families in the future.

MANDY: In other words …

JOHN-CAMPBELL: I'm not calling off the marriage if that's what you think I'm doing.

MANDY: Then what have you just said?

JOHN-CAMPBELL: Grandpa told me many stories. One stood out because it happened only a few months ago. Mazi Ogbuawa was a titled man in a village, not very far from ours. He had four children, three of them were girls and the last child was a boy. Mazi lost his wife before his third daughter's marriage, the first two were married years before the third. All of them left their husbands' homes the same day.

MANDY: (*Surprised.*) How?

(*The lights on stage A fade out slowly. Bright lights come up immediately on stage B, revealing a sitting-room in MAZI's house. The room is well furnished and decorated, depicting MAZI's status as a wealthy chief. Three sofas are arranged in the centre of the stage – a two-seater one is in between a single-seater one on the left and another on the right. A small centre table is placed right in front of the two-seater sofa. MAZI enters and walks up to the frame of his new wife hung on the wall, he tilts it up a bit and moves to sit on his two-seater sofa. He is wearing a short pair of trousers that stops at or above his knees and a close-fitting pullover shirt. He is a retired civil servant in his early sixties. There is a knock on the door.)*

MAZI: (*Sitting relaxed.*) Who's there?

EZIGBO: (*From backstage.*) It's Ezigbo, from Lagos.

MAZI: (*Surprised.*) Ah, my in-law … Please, come in. (*Rising up.*)

(Enter EZIGBO and CHINEME. They are dressed in the same traditional attire. EZIGBO has a red cap on his head while his wife has a headtie on. EZIGBO steps on the stage, rolling a leather suitcase behind him.)

CHINEME: (*Happily.*) Good afternoon, Father. (*She moves closer to MAZI to hug him.*)

MAZI: (*Smiling, rising.*) You're welcome, Neme. (*Hugs CHINEME.*)

EZIGBO: Good afternoon, my in-law. (*Shaking hands with MAZI.*) How are you doing?

MAZI: We are doing well, my in-law … You can see me, I'm fresher than ever before.

EZIGBO: Very good, my in-law. (*Smiles.*)

MAZI: Please, sit down, my children. (*They all sit down; CHINEME sits on the same sofa with MAZI, EZIGBO sits on the sofa on the left.*)

EZIGBO: Thank you, Sir.

MAZI: (*To CHINEME.*) How are you, my daughter?

CHINEME: (*Smiling.*) I'm fine, Papa.

MAZI: Let me get you people something to drink. Your throats must be dry by now. Lagos is far.

EZIGBO: No, don't worry, my in-law. We had something to drink and eat on our way.

MAZI: (*Refusing.*) Nooooo, my in-law. You can't come this far and not take anything. (*Rising up.*) Please, give me three minutes … (*Exit* MAZI.)

EZIGBO: (*To* CHINEME.) I hope you didn't forget to pack your international passport?

CHINEME: (*Nodding.*) No, it's in the suitcase.

EZIGBO: Okay.

(*Enter* MAZI, *whistling as he carries a plastic plate filled with garden eggs and kola nuts.*)

MAZI: My children … (*Placing the plate on the centre table.*) Here is kola.

EZIGBO: Thank you, my in-law.

MAZI: (*Sitting.*) So, what brings you people here on a week day? I'm really surprised to see you on a Tuesday.

EZIGBO: Yes, my in-law. I'm not surprised that you are surprised. I don't usually visit during the week because I have to go to the office. I had to come today anyway. My boss travelled abroad yesterday … so I decided to use the time.

MAZI: Okay.

EZIGBO: (*Sitting up.*) We hear you have a new wife now.

MAZI: (*Smiling.*) Yes, my in-law. I didn't want to trouble you, my children, to leave your business and come home because of a small thing. We just did a little ceremony.

EZIGBO: (*Nods.*) Okay.

MAZI: In fact, my wife is bringing some drinks for you people. She'll be here shortly.

EZIGBO: Okay.

(*Enter* NGOZI, *a beautiful, light-skinned, middle-aged*

woman dressed in a colourful traditional attire. She carries a plastic tray containing two glass cups and a pack of orange juice.)

MAZI: (*Excited.*) Here she comes … (*Talking to* EZIGBO *and* CHINEME.) You know her already.

CHINEME: (*To* NGOZI.) Good afternoon, Aunty (*Smiling.*)

NGOZI: How are you, Chineme?

CHINEME: I am fine.

NGOZI: (*To* EZIGBO.) And you, Ezigbo?

EZIGBO: I am doing well, as you can see.

NGOZI: (*Places the tray on the centre table.*) Welcome.

EZIGBO: Thank you.

NGOZI: I was roasting some meat in the kitchen before you came. You'd have to excuse me for some time, let me return to it. I'll join you when I'm done.

MAZI: It's okay, my dear. I hope they will taste your meat before they leave. (*Everyone smiles simultaneously.*)

NGOZI: Of course, they will.

MAZI: Okay. You may go then.

NGOZI: (*To* EZIGBO *and* CHINEME.) Welcome. (*Exit* NGOZI.)

EZIGBO: My in-law, it is because of your wife that we have come to see you.

MAZI: (*Excitedly surprised.*) Oh, but you didn't have to travel this far to congratulate us.

EZIGBO: We had to, my in-law. You know, when a tsetse fly perches on one's scrotum, it takes great skill to kill it, not force.

MAZI: (*More interested.*) That is true.

EZIGBO: Many people from this village called me to express

shock when you married Ngozi.

MAZI: (*Surprised.*) Eh heh … About what?

EZIGBO: My in-law, no matter how far one urinates, the last always falls at one's feet. We all know that Ngozi is not free to marry into any freeborn family.

MAZI: What are you saying, Ezigbo?

EZIGBO: I am trying to avoid calling a spade a spade. We all know that Ngozi is *osu* and there are consequences for marrying an *osu*.

MAZI: And do such consequences affect you and your household? Why not let me live with the consequences and manage them myself?

EZIGBO: My in-law, I am surprised that you are pretending to not know about the traditions of our people. I sat here in this room some years ago, when Mama was still alive … Here you advised a young man not to marry an *osu* girl. You recounted the consequences of doing that. You told him how far such marriage would go to affect him, his family and their unborn children.

MAZI: (*Nods in agreement.*) Yes.

EZIGBO: So, I have come to return your daughter, Chineme, to your family.

(MAZI *and* CHINEME *are shocked.*)

CHINEME: What is wrong with you, Ezigbo?

EZIGBO: (*To* MAZI.) I would normally ask that you return the bride price I paid when I came to marry your daughter, but I'd avoid such drama because I have to leave now. But I will pretend that you have returned all I paid for your daughter's hand. Please, I can't live with the consequences of your actions. While I love your daughter too much, I also love my children and I do not want them or their unborn children to suffer hardship or societal segregation because of the action you decided to take on your own, without considering its effect on others, especially those that are close to you.

MAZI: (*Looks at* EZIGBO *and* CHINEME in surprise.) I do not understand what you are saying, Ezigbo.

EZIGBO: I have made myself clear enough, Chief. I do not want to be in any marriage contract with your daughter or any member of your family.

MAZI: (*Looks at* CHINEME.) Did you agree to leave your husband's house?

CHINEME: Papa, I am as surprised as you are. Ezigbo didn't tell me what was up his sleeves. He just asked me to pack some things that we were coming to see you. I had no idea this was what he planned.

EZIGBO: (*Rising up.*) I am very sorry. I have no other choice. I must leave now.

(*Attempts to exit as lights fade. Bright lights return to stage A.*)

JOHN-CAMPBELL: All three men who married Mazi's daughters visited him one by one to return his daughters and collect their bride price, because Mazi had married an *osu* woman. Most elders in his extended family openly warned him against marrying Ngozi, but he was unwavering and desirous to marry his new sweetheart who stayed by his side for the nearly two years he had been a widower. According to Papa, Mazi's daughters currently shuttle between home and Lagos in the hope of saving their marriages and reuniting with their children. And as things stand now, Mazi is caught between breaking up with his new wife and performing a cleansing ceremony to rid him of the stigma and watching the marriages of his daughters disintegrate.

MANDY: The reason you've just narrated this is for me to see how far marrying me could affect you and your family, I am sure.

JOHN-CAMPBELL: Not that alone.

MANDY: What else is there?

JOHN-CAMPBELL: We must make sure that we are able to live with the consequences of our action. This is why I think that we must be sure that we love each other two hundred per cent. Anything short of that wouldn't be worth it.

MANDY: (*Surprised.*) You don't love me two hundred per cent?

JOHN-CAMPBELL: (*Shaking his head in disagreement.*) I never said anything like that, sweetheart.

MANDY: (*Crying slightly.*) So what do you mean?

JOHN-CAMPBELL: (*Concerned.*) My love, all I've said is that we should be patient a little.

MANDY: How can someone with all the education you have speak in this manner? You know, I don't know what has gotten into you these few days you've stayed in this village. In short … (*Rises up angrily and exits into the house.* JOHN-CAMPBELL *follows behind her. Lights fade.*)

Scene Five

Lights come on stage A. PAPA is seen polishing his brown sandals and listening to a small, black world receiver radio. Enter ELDER TIMOTHY, an old man of the same age as PAPA.

ELDER TIMOTHY: (*Giggling to* PAPA.) The old man himself.

PAPA: (*Surprised.*) Elder Timothy. (*Smiles.*)

ELDER TIMOTHY: This is how close we've become. I no longer have to knock on the door to come into your house. Why are you polishing your shoes with all that muscle?

PAPA: (*Laugh.*) Did I borrow some from you?

(*They both laugh.*)

Please, have your seat, my friend.

ELDER TIMOTHY: I will sit even if you don't offer me a seat. (*Sits beside* PAPA.)

PAPA: My grandson is around. He returned yesterday.

ELDER TIMOTHY: (*Not surprised at all.*) I heard. That's why I came. We hear he returned with an *osu*.

PAPA: (*Shocked.*) But he won't marry her.

ELDER TIMOTHY: (*Sarcastically.*) You have to be sure of that, my friend. Children are strong-willed these days, especially those who have lived in America and Europe for a long time.

PAPA: (*Firmly.*) He won't.

ELDER TIMOTHY: I know we preach to our church people to love their neigbours as themselves, but this *osu* matter is bigger than that. You know the consequences. You must try to stop this boy from pouring trouble on your head. This thing is still very serious and I'm sure that members of your family are already meeting in groups to discuss this matter because the news is all over the place.

(Suddenly, JOHN-CAMPBELL *and* MANDY *can be heard arguing backstage.* PAPA *and* ELDER TIMOTHY *sit quietly and listen to the loud argument between the two.)*

MANDY: I can't believe you and your people are behaving like this. I cannot. My father was supposed to leave his university next week and fly down to Nigeria so that he can arrange for my people to receive yours and you people are saying things from all corners of your mouth.

JOHN-CAMPBELL: Please, calm down, Chimamanda.

MANDY: Do you have to call me that? Obviously, something has gotten into your head.

JOHN-CAMPBELL: Is that no longer your name? Please, let us stop shouting. My grandfather can hear us.

MANDY: Let him hear. He's the cause of all this. How can we travel this far to get married only to have you quit because some village people have fed your ears with old stories?

JOHN-CAMPBELL: Mandy, I haven't agreed with my people yet.

MANDY: Yet?

JOHN-CAMPBELL: Look, you knew about this *osu* caste thing and you didn't tell me. Yet, you talk against keeping secrets. If you had told me about this while we were in the States, maybe we would have saved ourselves from all these embarrassments. Now, I'm only suggesting that we hold the marriage off for some time until we clear things up.

MANDY: Clear what thing up? I see you're no longer interested in this marriage. My father has a more befitting house in my village. I'm off.

JOHN-CAMPBELL: Please, Mandy. We can't behave like this now.

(Enter MANDY with her luggage – same luggage she came in with – angrily moving to the exit door. JOHN-CAMPBELL walks beside her, he tries to plead with her to stay. PAPA and ELDER TIMOTHY remain quiet for some time.)

Please, don't leave like this. It's already four o'clock. We can settle amicably, please.

MANDY: *(Dragging her luggage.)* This marriage is over.

(Exit.)

ELDER TIMOTHY: *(Rising up and walking to JOHN-CAMPBELL by the door.)* Let her go, my son. This happens all the time. Please, come and sit down.

(JOHN-CAMPBELL is sober. He walks to the chair and they sit down together.)

You see, my son, in this part of the world men don't commit suicide when a woman leaves, instead we should celebrate our freedom once more … the opportunity to go back into the wife market and take another one.

(Gesturing with his right hand.)

We have too many beautiful girls in this village. Obedient. Intelligent. They can cook, more than any girl you will find in America. You will find a better wife here, so don't worry about the one who just left.

PAPA: *(Looks at JOHN-CAMPBELL and ELDER TIMOTHY, then faces the audience.)* Life is like riding a bicycle, to keep your balance you must keep moving.

(Lights fade out slowly.)

– CURTAIN –

A Wife for My Husband

August, 2012

Characters

NNEBUOGOR	—	*Widow and mother of Nwandu and Chizitere*
VALERIA	—	*Nnebuogor's co-wife*
NWANDU	—	*Nnebuogor's first daughter*
CHIZITERE	—	*Twenty-three-year-old maiden*
ONOCHIE	—	*Nwandu's husband*
IWEGBU	—	*Nnebuogor's brother-in-law*
EZEULU	—	*Iwegbu's younger brother*
ULAEVUCHI	—	*Nnebuogor's friend and gossip*
ONWUAMAIBE	—	*Ulaevuchi's husband*
AFAMDI	—	*Chizitere's suitor*

An imaginary village in Eastern Nigeria. The play is set in the early 1980s.

Scene One

NNEBUOGOR's compound, in front of the house. It's very early in the morning. The compound is dirty, with dry leaves and goat droppings scattered here and there. An old basket, filled with dry leaves can be seen at one corner of the stage, with hoes and cutlasses beside it. The sound of birds chirping from a nearby tree can be heard onstage. One or two cocks crow from a distance. The stage suddenly becomes quiet. After three seconds, the sound of an electric radio comes on from backstage. It is an Igbo Christian song. NNEBUOGOR's voice is heard backstage, singing along with the music. She only recently converted to Christianity from traditional religion. In between NNEBUOGOR's music, the voice of IWEGBU is heard from backstage. He is whistling a tune. The sound of his melody gradually increases as he gets closer to stage. At the entrance, he stops whistling abruptly. IWEGBU appears onstage with his old, rickety bicycle and a wooden cane hanging at the back of his bicycle. He moves the bicycle close to the basket of leaves, leaning it against the wall; he uses his right leg to adjust the front tyre and picks his cane. IWEGBU is an old man in his seventies. His hair is grey; and the little beard under his chin and his moustache are all white.

IWEGBU: (*Cleaning his face with his right hand, he calls.*) Nnebuogor!

(*The music backstage immediately goes off. He calls again.*)

Oriaku!

NNEBUOGOR: (*Answers from backstage.*) Yes, Nna'anyi.

(*Enters quickly from the middle door. Surprised and genuflecting.*)

Good morning, Sir!

IWEGBU: Eh heh, Nnebuogor. How are you?

NNEBUOGOR: We are fine, my husband. We've managed to build back the fence behind the house and the kitchen wall. I hope that my goats and poultry won't catch the eye of thieves again.

(*She moves to the other corner of the stage to bring a wooden bench for* IWEGBU.) We have a seat, Nna'anyi.

(*She drops the bench directly behind him.*)

IWEGBU: Thank you.

(IWEGBU *sits as he draws out a chewing stick from his breast pocket and puts it in his mouth.*) Eh heh!

(*He puts his cane between his legs and looks away from* NNEBUOGOR. *He starts chewing his stick.*)

NNEBUOGOR: (*Calm and bold.*) What brings my in-law this early?

(*She sits on the same bench, at the edge of the other end.*) Is everything well with my in-law?

IWEGBU: (*Facing* NNEBUOGOR.) Oriaku!

NNEBUOGOR: (*Answering.*) Nna'anyi.

IWEGBU: Where is your daughter?

NNEBUOGOR: She is inside, in-law. Still sleeping.

IWEGBU: (*Sarcastically.*) Hmn!

NNEBUOGOR: I hope everything is all right, my husband?

IWEGBU: (*Sternly.*) All right?

(*Holds his right ear with his thumb and index finger.*) Nnebuogor! You do not ask a caged antelope what is wrong with it.

(*Leaving his ear.*) Didn't Emenike die over two years ago? Are you blind not to see what has become of his farmlands? All have been covered by weeds. You've abandoned them; for how long now? Last time, the cassava and corn fell into the hands of thieves, who know not their left from the right, because Nnebuogor has become too weak and lazy to cultivate! Have I complained? A shut mouth is often a wise one! I have watched you and your daughter move around like big birds, lavishing my brother's wealth and expending all the monies you collect from his tenants, as if you are Queen Eliza of Great Britain. Every evening, you would accompany Obiageli's daughter to the Church and trouble the entire village with your noise in the worship of your new God. That is not a problem for me o! But in the end, you drop all my brother worked for his entire life in their little black box. I, Iwegbu, son of Obidigbo, the great lion of Umuezike, accompanied my brother to pay your bride price, and I know how much your head cost my people. In case you have forgotten, Emenike emptied his barn to marry you. I lent him five hundred naira, Mazi Ezeulu, two hundred, just to make your people happy.

(*Pointing in no definite direction.*)

All the goats and chickens Emenike reared for some time, we slaughtered to please the long throats of your people. Didn't we bring over eight gallons of wine to your people? Yet, you people watched him die without becoming a man.

NNEBUOGOR: (*Surprised.*) A man?

IWEGBU: Yes. Do you pretend not to know that Emenike joined his ancestors without an heir, one who would preserve his lineage? All the members of his family have not given up hope. We still wait to hear the cry of a son!

NNEBUOGOR: (*Amazed.*) I am surprised, my husband. What do you mean?

(*Looking at her stomach.*) I am not pregnant. I can't be. Did my husband not die two years ago? Has my in-law forgotten already that Emenike lies there, in the ground?

(*Pointing to another end of the stage, she continues.*) Under

Mama's favourite *ukwa* tree …

IWEGBU: (*Clearing his throat.*) Nnebuogor! Our people always say that a family without an elderly person does not know the difference between day and night!

NNEBUOGOR: (*Nodding.*) True.

IWEGBU: (*Nods abruptly and hits his cane slowly on the ground three times.*) A man's honour is not his belongings but his children!

NNEBUOGOR: Also true, my in-law.

IWEGBU: You know that at least. (*Pointing to the house with his cane.*) So what will happen to this compound and the buildings in it when you join Emenike to meet your ancestors in the other life? Or you don't think you will?

NNEBUOGOR: (*Looking around the compound.*) Nothing will happen, my in-law.

IWEGBU: (*Hits his cane on the ground once.*) Nothing?

NNEBUOGOR: Do you expect something to happen, my in-law? Nwandu and Chizitere have grown big enough to clean this place. Both of them are older than I was when I married your brother. They are mature enough to make sure that this building doesn't fall, even if I die today.

IWEGBU: And so?

NNEBUOGOR: They helped their father a great deal each time he went on to work in the farm. Chizitere has been my eyes since he died. She does most of the chores in this house.

IWEGBU: (*Mockingly.*) And she is still sleeping?

NNEBUOGOR: Yes, Nna'anyi. She fetched water all through the evening, yesterday. She filled all the drums at the backyard before she had her evening meal. She even managed to go to church after her meal to join her mates in preparing for the youth vigil.

(*Unconcerned.*) So, I asked her not to bother waking up

early today. What is she getting up early to do again?

IWEGBU: (*Nodding slowly.*) Eh heh! Is that so?

NNEBUOGOR: Yes, my in-law. There's no outstanding housework.

IWEGBU: Will Chizitere not marry tomorrow?

NNEBUOGOR: (*Claps her hands as she remembers something.*) That reminds me.

(*Changing the subject.*)

My in-law, you remember Afamdi, Chizitere's suitor? He and his people shall be coming to see you whenever you approve.

IWEGBU: (*Fiercely.*) Shut up, Woman! Approve what? Is that what I have come here to talk about?

NNEBUOGOR: (*Kneels on the ground and sits back immediately.*) Pardon me, my in-law. I should have come after noon yesterday to give you this information, but for the little rain that made the soil so slippery in the morning. I even fell flat on my buttocks while trying to move firewood away from the hut into the kitchen because of the wet ground. I should have come yesterday.

IWEGBU: (*Shouts in disgust.*) Shhh! You still talk about things with no relevance to the reason I left my house this morning.

(*Turning away.*) Don't force my hand, Nnebuogor. Your daughter is not why I have come here today. I did not leave my house before the last cock crow to come and mingle with or laugh away the troubles of this family.

(*Looks up.*) All of us cannot sleep and place our heads in one direction. No bird, none at all, flies with just one wing! Just like a man who does not marry, a man without a son, owes a lot to his family.

NNEBUOGOR: (*As if serious, she rubs her hands and adjusts her buttocks on the bench, leaning forward.*) My in-law must be here for an important reason then. It was not my intention to offend you. Forgive my tongue. I am a woman. My mouth speaks before my head reasons. But, my feet are shaking.

(*She looks at her feet simultaneously with* IWEGBU). I did not bear a male child for my husband.

(*Affectionately.*) But I know how much he cherished Nwandu.

IWEGBU: And is she not in her husband's house today?

NNEBUOGOR: Yes. But she comes every other day to assist us in doing one or two things here, especially on the days her husband is absent. He still visits Onitsha every week to buy goods for his shop. Sometimes he sleeps at his in-law's place in Onitsha. So, Nwandu relocates to run away from loneliness.

IWEGBU: Nwandu cannot always be here. It is simple. She is not a man. She owes all the duties of womanhood to her husband and his family, not to us. So, she cannot be a man or perform the functions of one.

NNEBUOGOR: (*Smiling lightly.*) My in-law, you forget how you used to tease Nwandu while she was growing up, telling her that she had all the strength of a man. Everybody knows that about Nwandu. She can do whatever a man can …

IWEGBU: (*Cutting in angrily.*) Can she impregnate a woman? A lizard may look like a crocodile, but they are not the same; they can never be the same!

NNEBUOGOR: But …

IWEGBU: (*Cuts in.*) I must be too old. Maybe I should speak clearly, and like a child for you to understand and talk less frequently about these children of yours.

NNEBUOGOR: (*Resignedly.*) Maybe. Maybe, our husband.

IWEGBU: (*Firmly.*) It has become obvious since Emenike died that all of you had no love for him, when he was alive and even now that he is dead. You people have depleted his yam barns.

(*Pointing in no definite direction.*) All the palm trees the great palm wine tapper tapped for your husband have suddenly withered. Look at his compound, can you not see that this place is dirty? It has been like this since the man died. True or false?

(*He continues, as if ignoring* NNEBUOGOR.) Look.

(*Pointing to the house behind him with his cane.*) See the house Emenike rubbed white chalk annually on, before each new yam festival; it is beginning to look like red mud. You can't paint it? Termites would have started eating up the canes holding the roof, just like your kitchen behind the house, which fell to the ground some days ago because of the same neglectful attitude you people have had towards my late brother's estate. We have obviously become tired of watching this nonsense happen. I am not interested in Emenike's belongings o! But the truth must be told at all times. No tree is known by its roots, but by its fruits. Before we all know it, your remaining daughter will marry and then you will join your ancestors. Then, my brother and his name will be snuffed from the face of the earth just like that, because all of us failed to do what was necessary to save his lineage from extinction.

NNEBUOGOR: (*Shaking her head in disagreement.*) Not so, not so, my in-law. Chizitere and her husband, whoever he becomes, shall continue with my husband's lineage. They will have as many children as they want, more than we ever had. We have not stopped praying for Nwandu and her husband.

IWEGBU: (*With a rebuff.*) Shut up, Nnebuogor! Maybe you should be quiet sometimes.

(*Slowly shaking his head in pity.*) Poor Emenike.

(*Beating his chest quietly.*) I am sure he would have tumbled three times in his grave in regret of this nonsense your mouth just uttered.

(*He looks away and spits.*) Tufia! Women! You said it before. You speak before your head begins to reason. At least, you know that.

NNEBUOGOR: (*Nodding in agreement.*) My in-law, I was only reminding you that we have two wonderful daughters. Your people say that a man without shoes is better than one without legs.

IWEGBU: (*Cuts in.*) And a cow without a tail will soon be mocked by little flies. You, especially, have in fact turned this family into a laughing stock, a tool for gossip by women like you. You of all people should know that women do not share of their father's bequest but their mother's, just as men have nothing to do with that of their mothers. Even though my brother had written a will before he died, distributing his properties to your daughters, the ownership of this compound is the prerogative of his first son. A man, not a woman! A boy can only inherit this house, not those daughters you make noise about.

NNEBUOGOR: (*Forlornly, with tears in her eyes.*) My in-law, I am not barren. I was never unfruitful for my husband. You know that I had three boys before Nwandu and Chizitere. Is it my fault that all of them died of measles and cholera? Or is it my fault that I have become too old, old that my husband and I couldn't have more children after trying so hard for a long time before his sudden, sad death?

(*Mournful.*) Death! What should I begin to throw these blames at, old age or death?

(*Holding her head.*) What would an old widow like me do in such circumstance?

IWEGBU: Oriaku, it is too late to start crying over a cup of wine that has been spilled. Emenike is dead. We cannot start looking behind our backs. But we must move on from here now to grow his lineage.

(*Clearing his throat.*) That's why I am here.

NNEBUOGOR: Words! You must be tired of words, my in-law. (*Stands up.*) I must run inside to get you kola and wine to soothe your throat.

IWEGBU: (*Calling her back with his hands.*) Leave that one, Woman.

NNEBUOGOR: Are you sure, Nna'anyi?

IWEGBU: Sit down. (NNEBUOGOR *sits.*) You see, it has been two years. For those two years, I haven't bothered to bring this up until now. I thought you were as wise as our mother, who always reasoned like a man. My brother always told some of us, his kinsmen, that you were as wise as Mama. Sometimes, I wonder where all the wisdom he talked about has gone. I expected you to come forward to his family, on your own, with a strategy to give Emenike a son.

NNEBUOGOR: (*Holding her head high. With calm.*) Hmn ...

IWEGBU: Anyway, I haven't come to confirm my brother's assertions. But it is tradition to see that his lineage continues to grow after his demise. And, as his eldest brother and head of this family, I have decided to come to you as a mark of respect. After long thoughts and gnashing away my weak teeth for many nights, I have come up with the best solution to dealing with this problem. I think that it is necessary for Emenike to take another wife.

NNEBUOGOR: (*Shocked.*) Another wife?

IWEGBU: (*Slowly hits his cane on the ground.*) Yes, a second wife!

NNEBUOGOR: (*Still shocked.*) Nna'anyi, I don't mean to be

rude. I don't know you to be a man who drinks too much wine, if not I would think you are under the influence of it. But I will ask, how do you expect Emenike to marry a second wife after his death? Or are we talking about another Emenike who isn't my husband?

IWEGBU: (*Firmly.*) Nnebuogor! When Emenike came to me to say that he wanted to marry a beautiful girl from Amakohia, I warned him about the troubles that would follow marrying from another village. Those problems have already begun to manifest. How can you pretend not to know what I'm talking about? Is thirty-three years or so not time enough for you to learn about some aspects of our traditions? I warned him.

(*Nodding.*) I warned Emenike. But he wouldn't listen! You see.

(*Looking up and away from* NNEBUOGOR.) The mosquito that refused the counsel of the wise one will soon follow the corpse to the grave.

NNEBUOGOR: My in-law, what do we need a second wife or a son for?

IWEGBU: Nnebuogor!

(*Holding his right ear.*) Be careful! A bird is caught by its wings, a woman by her tongue. Be careful!

NNEBUOGOR: Nna'anyi Iwegbu, please, tell me. Maybe I don't know. What else will a male child do for us? What would he do that is beyond my children's abilities as women? Have they done anything to embarass this family? Chizitere is loved by everyone. She rarely comes home without a gift or favour each time she goes out. The other day, she came home with a new pot, given to her by an elderly woman because she broke hers. A classic moonlight tale, isn't it? Even in the Church, she has become one of the leaders of the youth gathering. She sings, she preaches the words of our Lord. Yes, she is a woman. But, is she not better than ten male children? What about Nwandu? The same thing before she moved to her husband's house.

IWEGBU: (*Laughs sarcastically*.) A ripe fruit will not hang forever on a tree branch. Soon and very soon, mark my words, this Chizitere you talk about then and again, would marry and become her husband's family, their pride, their property not ours, just like Nwandu, whom you also mentioned ... then, Emenike's lineage will come to an end just like that o! Was it not you who talked about Chizitere's suitors coming to see me? (*Sarcastically.*) Were you referring to another Chizitere, who isn't your daughter?

NNEBUOGOR: The same Chizitere, my in-law.

IWEGBU: (*Concerned.*) Time is not our friend. Chizitere's breasts are full and ripe. All the young men in this village will soon turn my house into a pilgrimage centre. Before that begins to happen, we must bring in a second wife for Emenike, one that would give him a son. This son will grow Emenike's lineage, preserve it, and see to it that the walls of this house remain firm and the compound free from all forms of weed or intruders.

NNEBUOGOR: (*Confused.*) You are not very clear, my in-law. Your words still come out strange.

IWEGBU: Strange? (*Chuckles.*) I will say no more, Nnebuogor. Maybe you should go and ask your fellow women if it is just right for you to ignore the fact that Emenike had no son while he was alive. And if it is proper for you and your children to maintain the status quo. You should stop behaving as if you are ignorant of our tradition. I am leaving you now. (*Rising.*)

NNEBUOGOR: (*Hesitant, getting up.*) All right, my in-law.

IWEGBU: (*Moving to take his bicycle from the wall.*) Go and ask questions about our traditions, so that you know what our people do in this kind of situation. You can't just sit here and behave as if you don't care about what happens to your husband's name. Go and find out. A traveller who asks questions does not miss his way.

NNEBUOGOR: I will, in-law.

IWEGBU: (*Exiting the stage slowly with his bicycle.*) I will meet with my kinsmen and call you when we are ready. We will send a message across to you.

NNEBUOGOR: (*Smiling facetiously.*) Go well, Nna'anyi. Greet your family for me, especially Aunty.

(NNEBUOGOR *stands for a while with her finger in her mouth. She sits down slowly on the bench as if thinking.*) What is the meaning of this?

(*Acts as if asking the audience.*) Why won't they leave me alone? Men!

(*Puts her hands over her head and snaps her fingers.*) May God forbid!

(*Immediately,* ULAEVUCHI *enters, appearing untidy with scattered hair. She is wearing a white shirt on a wrapper tied just above her breasts.*)

ULAEVUCHI: My sister, good morning o.

NNEBUOGOR: Good morning, Ula.

ULAEVUCHI: (*Rather concerned.*) Is it not too early in the morning for you to be looking confused, as if your house is on fire? Where is Chizitere?

NNEBUOGOR: She is inside, sleeping.

ULAEVUCHI: I am running to buy some *akamu* and *akara* for Onwuamaibe.

(*Smiles.*) Trying to be a good wife for the man, like you.

(*Contemplatively walking away. Talks to herself.*) I hope all is well.

NNEBUOGOR: It's all right. Go well, my sister.

ULAEVUCHI: (*Attempting to leave stage from the opposite exit.*) Thank you.

NNEBUOGOR: I must come and see you when Chizitere wakes up. Something bothers me, *biko*.

ULAEVUCHI: (*Exiting stage.*) Till then, Nne'm.

NNEBUOGOR: (*A long pause as she remains on the bench, wondering.*) Hmn!

(*Calling out.*) Chizitere.

CHIZITERE: (*From backstage.*) Yes, Ma.

(*Enters. She comes before* NNEBUOGOR *and yawns with her right hand covering her mouth.*) Nne, good morning.

NNEBUOGOR: Good morning, Zizi. Please, get me my medicine. You will see it on the floor, behind the bed … the black liquid in the whisky bottle which dorkitor gave me on Saturday.

CHIZITERE: (*Exit briefly. Returns with a small bottle of black liquid.*) Here, Nne. (*Hands bottle to* NNEBUOGOR.)

NNEBUOGOR: Thank you.

(CHIZITERE *leaves stage sleepily, seeming to count her steps.* NNEBUOGOR *sighs heavily as she pours some of the liquid content from the bottle unto its cover. She gulps down her medicine. A quick fade.*)

Scene Two

A faint lantern light reveals a room in ONWUAMAIBE's house. The room is ONWUAMAIBE's parlour. ULAEVUCHI is lying on a three-pillow chair, with her head on the chair's arm. Like a pillow, her right hand is behind her head. Another single chair, similar to the one she rests on can be seen at the adjacent corner. The decoration in the room is modest. A large bow and arrow adorns one side of the wall. Empty beer bottles and a glass cup placed over the mouth of a palm wine keg can be seen below a wooden table at another corner of the room. A loud, continuous knock is heard on the door.

ULAEVUCHI: (*Opens eyes and looks at the door.*) Ha!

> (*Standing up. She increases the brightness of the lantern and walks towards the door.*) This man and his *wahala*. (*Opening door.*)

NNEBUOGOR: (*Enters and goes straight to sit on the single chair. She is moody and temperamental.*) Ula, I don't understand your people o!

ULAEVUCHI: (*Dazed.*) What?

NNEBUOGOR: (*Rather exasperated.*) I don't understand my husband's people, his brother especially.

ULAEVUCHI: (*A bit relieved.*) Hmn! I thought it was Onwuamaibe who hit the door like he was going to break it.

> (*She moves close to NNEBUOGOR and sits on the chair she lay on earlier.*) As usual, he left this house since noon to join his fellow pot-bellied friends to drink wine, eat pepper soup and make jest of themselves in the open public.

NNEBUOGOR: (*Calmly.*) At least, you have a husband whose presence you feel.

ULAEVUCHI: Is it enough to feel my husband's presence? Of

what good is a man who drinks himself to stupor until he loses control of his common sense?

NNEBUOGOR: He is still your husband, my sister.

ULAEVUCHI: Of course! A husband who lacks the basic ingredients of manhood. Who knows, the gods may have given him to me as punishment for my mouth.

NNEBUOGOR: Is it that bad?

ULAEVUCHI: My mouth or my husband?

NNEBUOGOR: Both.

ULAEVUCHI: Hmn! You didn't hear about the havoc I caused in my neighbour's compound last *Afo* day?

NNEBUOGOR: What havoc?

ULAEVUCHI: The news spread like wildfire.

NNEBUOGOR: What happened? What did you do?

ULAEVUCHI: (*Dramatically.*) Can you imagine? This woman has been saying all sorts of rubbish and yelling insults at me.

(*Mimicking.*) I have no children, I have no child. She forgets that I have a keen ear.

(*Narratively.*) She wouldn't wake up any morning without calling Ulaevuchi's name. I have warned her several times but her ears are as thick as palm kernel, too hard to pick a stern warning. Am I the only barren woman in this village? From my room, the other day, I heard some people gossiping about me and it originated from her compound. I came out and saw her pointing to my house and telling stories to some ugly women gathered in one corner. When I moved closer, I heard them say my name. I finished them, insulted daylight and night out of them. I cursed them to their last generations.

(*She spreads her legs and puts the tip of her wrapper between them and begins to swing them carelessly, now and then.*)

Trust me, I didn't forget their forebears. They don't know who I am. I know the secrets of every dead and living being in this village. I exposed all of them that day and all the dirty things they had said about the other neighbours. Come and see talk.

NNEBUOGOR: (*Concerned.*) Was all that necessary?

ULAEVUCHI: Necessary? Yes o! That woman wants to try me; over my dead body, then my name is not Ula.

NNEBUOGOR: But you didn't fight with them?

ULAEVUCHI: Did I say that? Any head that knocks the beehive bears the sting. I tore my neighbour's blouse and almost skinned her partner naked.

NNEBUOGOR: Ha!

ULAEVUCHI: Anyway, she was lucky that another neighbour came to her rescue and separated us. Was I mad! I was all giddy with joy. One of us would have seen our ancestors that harsh morning, true! It was when the old woman who separated us tried to make peace between us that I realised that they weren't talking about me. It was the farmer's wife who lives behind my house. But it appeared as if it was me, after all, they pointed fingers in my direction and talked about barreness.

NNEBUOGOR: (*Laughs.*) What? You see, things are not always the way they seem.

ULAEVUCHI: But then, they called my name. They were lucky. Their *chi* was with them that morning. I apologised. But that warning I gave them should scare them enough to never cross my path or step on my toe or anywhere around this compound again.

NNEBUOGOR: U-laaa-evuchi.

ULAEVUCHI: Yes, that is me. (*Beating her chest.*) The name

which says our god is not asleep and yet it has become a source of trouble to the neighbours.

NNEBUOGOR: (*Chuckles.*) You and *wahala*. You like trouble o!

ULAEVUCHI: Yes! It is me who would stay in my shell and give trouble to onlookers who wouldn't mind their business.

(*Changing the subject.*) So, what was bothering my sister this morning? Tell me, let me go and handle it for you. I know you don't fight like me. When you're quiet like this, people take you for granted. You become their fool every day. What is more, you have joined the Holy Mary people to shout hallelujah. Tell me …

NNEBUOGOR: (*Disgruntled.*) Look at my husband's brother; the one whose son sells headache medicine at *Afo*.

ULAEVUCHI: (*Cuts in.*) Iwegbu?

NNEBUOGOR: Yes. Iwegbu who rarely stepped his feet into my house or his eyes on me and my daughters after my husband died. Now he has become Emenike's next of kin, our caregiver. He now speaks for his gods and ancestors, and perhaps Emenike.

ULAEVUCHI: These men will always be the troubles of us. What did he do? That man's eyes have always been on Emenike's estate. Has he come to make you his second wife already?

NNEBUOGOR: What wife? Old me. What would an old rag offer him? He would never run after a woman with flattened breasts, not sensitive enough to please his heart or bring to life his fantasies. My waist is already too weak and fragile to turn his eyes. More so, Iwegbu has so many children who would prepare his meals and care for him and his wife when they've become too old to bathe themselves.

ULAEVUCHI: Eh heh …

NNEBUOGOR: He came to my house this morning to talk about some silly marriage proposal.

ULAEVUCHI: (*Listening.*) To whom? Chizitere?

NNEBUOGOR: (*With a sigh.*) Eh? He said he had perfected plans with his kinsmen to marry another wife for Emenike. Ask me, my sister, did Emenike not die over two years ago?

ULAEVUCHI: Oh! Don't mind them. They are not serious!

NNEBUOGOR: That's not the impression I got from his face. He wasn't smiling at all.

ULAEVUCHI: Wicked men! They've come to you with their bogus traditions.

NNEBUOGOR: What kind of tradition is this, my friend? Who marries for a dead man in this time and age? I know that some old customs allowed relations to marry for the dead in special circumstances. But I've never taken such customs seriously. How?

ULAEVUCHI: I have always told you that you are too soft to be trapped in this backward, good for nothing village.

NNEBUOGOR: What can a woman do in this village without her husband? Is he not everything?

ULAEVUCHI: Hmm, you know Egodinma, my former neighbour who married the butcher from the riverine village, close to our boundary with the Idemili thick forest? Her husband supplied the meat for our women's meeting some years ago …

NNEBUOGOR: (*Recalling.*) Yes. Her husband died some time ago. (*Thinking.*) Yes.

ULAEVUCHI: (*Listening.*) Yes, exactly, that one. Ego, tall and gigantic as she is, even with long arms and legs, couldn't fight her husband's people. You would see Ego even when she sits amongst giants. Yet, she is too weak, weaker than a day-old chicken and foolish to her bones. Her husband had barely rested in his six-foot grave when all his kinsmen descended on her because she had no child for the man.

Egodinma suffered, she suffered. She was beaten severely. They almost sent her to meet her ancestors. All of them accused her of tying her womb and killing her dear husband.

(*She belches.*) What did they not do to her? Before they buried his body, they locked her away in a dark room, starved her of food and on the day they released her …

(*Counting with her fingers.*) One, two, three, after seven whole days, they forced her to drink the smelly, dirty water that was used to wash her husband's corpse. All this drama was to test her innocence in her husband's death. You could feel Egodinma's sorrow from outside, even from a distant land. The poor, fragile widow, screaming, unable to sleep, unable to leave the room to even defecate or pass urine, she didn't see light for seven days, seven whole days. They said it was tradition to do this before they buried his corpse. If not, his spirit was to linger on until it found rest.

NNEBUOGOR: (*Dismayed.*) Ehh!

ULAEVUCHI: (*Nods slowly.*) Even when she came out alive, they continued to maltreat her as if she was a stranger to the family. One of her brothers-in-law was accused of raping her while she was confined to the dark room. People heard her scream on the night of the rape. If not for the intervention of one old man in her husband's family, she may have died that day. They had no reason to kill her, unless their intention was to send her to meet her husband.

NNEBUOGOR: (*Thankfully, looking up and raising her hands.*) May our good God be praised.

ULAEVUCHI: (*Mockingly.*) The gods be praised? Why are you praising God already? I haven't finished Egodinma's story, have I? Ironically, the same hunched-back old man, whom Egodinma thought was kind to have intervened, arranged a young maiden to marry her late husband.

NNEBUOGOR: (*Surprised. Covers her mouth with her right hand*.) Oh!

ULAEVUCHI: They hurriedly married the maiden for her husband and she was now to perform his social functions and care for this young wife. A man was contracted from a close-by village to perform the genital role and make this maiden pregnant. Egodinma now cares for two boys who came out of that ungodly marriage.

NNEBUOGOR: (*Still shocked*.) Jesus Christ! Is this not the same thing Nna'anyi Iwegbu is planning for my husband?

ULAEVUCHI: Yes. They will expect you to play the role of female father to the children from the new wife.

NNEBUOGOR: (*Disgusted, but calm*.) How I thought I married into a good family.

ULAEVUCHI: (*Mimicking*.) Good family. Sure!

NNEBUOGOR: (*Still disgusted*.) What can a widow do?

ULAEVUCHI: Nne, you are too quiet and gentle to match these people. Your new religion makes things worse. What did you do to the tomato hawker at *Afo* when she poured her paste on your white wrapper? Nothing! You just muttered a simple sorry because your Bible says that you should present your second cheek to your tormentor after he slaps you first. You apologised like a fool.

NNEBUOGOR: Should I have thrown dirty words on her or destroyed her goods in anger?

ULAEVUCHI: (*Eager*.) Yes! You should have done either of those. Ulaevuchi will always fight for you. These village men will not be our destruction. We must fight them when they treat us like filthy rags, or else, they begin to push one around like a little child. A rat whose house has been taken over by a snake does not know rest. So, you must fight! I am behind you. In short, no, I'm in front. When that old man comes to your house again, when he gets even close, call me. If not, this episode will end up like that of the tomato hawker and you won't be happy at all. When Iwegbu sees me, he and his kinsmen will run for safety, I am sure. You do not tell a child not to touch a hot lamp, the lamp will tell him. Nobody calls me trouble for nothing! Me and trouble, the same day, we were born.

(*There's a loud knock on the door which pauses for a while, then* ULAEVUCHI *and* NNEBUOGOR *look at each other. A loud knock is heard again.*)

ULAEVUCHI: (*Furious.*) Who?

ONWUAMAIBE: (*From outside, he sounds drunk.*) Open this door, Woman!

ULAEVUCHI: (*With rising temper.*) Can you imagine this man again?

(*Contemplating, then suddenly.*) Go back to your beer parlour. Go back. There you have found the comfort and satisfaction that you've deprived beautiful Ulaevuchi. Foolish man!

ONWUAMAIBE: (*Still outside and drunk.*) Open this door, U-laa!

NNEBUOGOR: (*Concerned.*) Please, allow him come inside so that he can wash his face and see well.

ULAEVUCHI: (*Making gestures for silence.*) Let him, a decaying plantain which thinks that it is ripening, go back there and drink off his miserable life.

NNEBUOGOR: (*Rising to open the door.*) Let me help you.

ULAEVUCHI: (*Holding her back.*) Not now, my sister. (*Rises, moving closer to the door.*) I will open this door because I know how much you fear the *eke*.

(NNEBUOGOR *sits down.* ULAEVUCHI *opens the door. Enter*

ONWUAMAIBE, *a middle-aged man in his fifties. He is wearing red chieftaincy regalia over a pair of black trousers and a red cap on his head. He holds a neatly carved cane as he staggers to the centre of the stage, right before* NNEBUOGOR.)

ONWUAMAIBE: (*Talking to* NNEBUOGOR.) Oh! Nne, you are here.

NNEBUOGOR: (*Rising.*) Welcome, Onwuamaibe. Welcome.

ONWUAMAIBE: Thank you, good woman. If we had two of you in this village, how can we then die of old age? Our gods made you well. You have a good heart, not like the woman I married.

ULAEVUCHI: (*Comes closer to* ONWUAMAIBE *from the door.*) Go! Soon, sleep will come. Why would a bad man not get a bad wife?

ONWUAMAIBE: (*Staggering to a middle exit.*) You see. So you know you are a bad wife? That is why I can marry only one wife. Another one of you would send me to my untimely death. Seriously ...

NNEBUOGOR: (*To* ONWUAMAIBE.) May God forbid!

ONWUAMAIBE: (*Attempting to exit.*) Ogor, sleep well. (*Exit.*)

ULAEVUCHI: (*Pointing to the middle exit.*) See! You have seen who I married. Yet, they say I am trouble. Our ancestors are not kind to have presented me this misery.

NNEBUOGOR: My sister, let me be on my way before the moonlight starts disappearing. I don't want to borrow your lantern.

ULAEVUCHI: Nne'm, no problem. I beg, don't forget to call me when that old, miserable man appears at your house again to talk about a second wife for your husband. The moment you see him, ask Chizitere to come and call me. It won't take a minute.

NNEBUOGOR: (*Going.*) Ulaevuchi! I'm not sure my in-law can stand your tongue. He is old and weak already. You want to kill him?

ULAEVUCHI: Then he should stay away from your compound and free you from this traditional nonsense. Shouldn't he?

NNEBUOGOR: Even if you had the power to stop them, what would you do? Make trouble? Your troubles will only make matters worse and not bring me out of the situation.

ULAEVUCHI: (*Bending to hear her.*) What?

NNEBUOGOR: But it is true, no lies.

ULAEVUCHI: (*Soft laughter.*) Well, my sister, even dirty water extinguishes fire. These men will not be our destruction. Not today. We won't sleep and die in their hands.

NNEBUOGOR: (*Less concerned.*) Sleep well, Ula.

ULAEVUCHI: (*Seeing her off to the door.*) Goodnight.

(*Exit* NNEBUOGOR. ULAEVUCHI *shuts the door. She moves centre stage, picks up the lantern and moves out from the middle exit. Slow fade.*)

Scene Three

Darkness. Light Igbo Christian music comes up from a radio backstage. NNEBUOGOR's voice is heard singing along with the music coming from the radio. Lights now come up, revealing NNEBUOGOR in her compound, before the same house, as in Scene One. It is just past noon. A wrapper is tied above her breasts and her shoulders are bare. She sits on a bamboo stool while sifting chaff from a small quantity of rice, placed in a tray on her lap. She continues singing. Enter CHIZITERE and AFAMDI. CHIZITERE is wearing a headtie over her plaited hair and a satin blouse over a very long skirt. AFAMDI, in his mid-twenties, holds CHIZITERE by the hand as they come onstage, but leaves her hand as they get closer to NNEBUOGOR, who sits centre stage.

CHIZITERE: (*Genuflecting.*) Mama, good afternoon.

AFAMDI: (*Greeting simultaneously with* CHIZITERE.) Good afternoon, Mama.

NNEBUOGOR: Eh heh, my children. You have come.

AFAMDI: Yes.

NNEBUOGOR: How was the practice at Father's house?

CHIZITERE: (*A bit excited.*) Fine, Mama. Afamdi was chosen to replace Ugo who joined the former parish priest to his new parish. Father said he had the strongest baritone voice in the group.

NNEBUOGOR: (*Excited.*) Ah ah, that's a very good one.

AFAMDI: Thank you, Mama.

NNEBUOGOR: I hope you know how tasking the job gets, especially during the harvests and bazaars.

AFAMDI: Yes, Mama.

NNEBUOGOR: This also means that you'll spend less time with Chizitere.

CHIZITERE: That is the bitter part.

AFAMDI: (*Sad face.*) Yes.

CHIZITERE: But it's alright. So long as he spends that time with Jesus. I do not mind sharing him with our Saviour. After all, he sent Afam to me. I won't be a selfish woman, especially with my husband.

NNEBUOGOR: Hmmm. You should be o, with your husband, or else another beautiful lady will win his love and attention just before your eyes.

AFAMDI: (*Shaking his head in disagreement.*) No, Mama. No other woman is beautiful enough to take my eyes away from Chizitere. She's everything any man could wish for. I can never ask for more.

CHIZITERE: (*Smiles.*) Thank you, Afam. That's why I can trust you with my life.

NNEBUOGOR: You children, eh ... you have become too bold. You should only say these things when you're alone.

CHIZITERE: Mama, do not mind Afam. Sometimes he loses control of his mind because of love.

AFAMDI: (*To* CHIZITERE.) Should you expect anything less?

NNEBUOGOR: It's okay. I am happy both of you are in love. It is not a bad thing.

AFAMDI: (*Seriously.*) Well, Mama, I don't know if you have discussed my family's planned visit with Uncle? I overheard some of my kinsmen talking about going to Nnobi for someone's funeral. I am not sure when they plan this trip. But I think it's important we try and fix a date early enough so that I can plan well with my people.

NNEBUOGOR: (*Nodding.*) Yes. Nna'anyi Iwegbu was here the

other day and we have discussed this matter. Sure, I must go and see him today because, like you said, it is important for us to fix a date now.

CHIZITERE: Then I may have to come with you, Mama, that way he'll know that we are serious.

AFAMDI: Yes, it'll appear so.

NNEBUOGOR: No. It won't do us much good to see him together. I will see him alone.

CHIZITERE: Okay.

AFAMDI: Thank you, Mama. I'll have to run back home now before it gets dark.

NNEBUOGOR: I know.

AFAMDI: But I'll come here tomorrow to know about the outcome of your discussion with Uncle.

NNEBUOGOR: That's fine, my son.

CHIZITERE: (*To* NNEBUOGOR.) I hope I can see him off to the road.

NNEBUOGOR: (*Nods briefly.*) Yes. Why not?

AFAMDI: I will see you tomorrow, Mama.

NNEBUOGOR: Go well, my dear.

(*Exit* AFAMDI *and* CHIZITERE. NNEBUOGOR *resumes sifting. After a while,* NWANDU's *voice is heard backstage.*)

NWANDU: (*From backstage.*) Mama.

NNEBUOGOR: (*Surprised.*) Nwandu.

(NWANDU *enters. She is also a young lady of about thirty years. She is wearing a long gown made from local fabric and a pair of sandals on her feet. She comes in carrying heavy luggage. She appears very tired from carrying the luggage.*)

NWANDU: Good afternoon, Mama.

NNEBUOGOR: (*Really shocked to see her with the luggage. She rises and moves up to* NWANDU.) Ah ah, what's the problem? Why are you carrying this bag alone?

NWANDU: (*Unconcerned.*) Don't worry yourself, Mama. Let us sit a little first. I am so tired. I had to drag this bag all by myself.

NNEBUOGOR: (*Pretends to be calm.*) Are you sure everything is alright, Nwandu?

NWANDU: Please, let us sit. Then, we can talk.

NNEBUOGOR: Okay, come

(NNEBUOGOR *attempts to carry* NWANDU's *luggage*).

NWANDU: Please, let me carry it alone. It's heavy.

NNEBUOGOR: Please, come and drop that bag here.

(*She leads* NWANDU *to a corner of the stage where they leave the luggage*). Come and sit, let us talk.

NWANDU: Thank you, Mama.

(*They sit down together on a wooden bench by* NNEBUOGOR's *bamboo stool.*)

NNEBUOGOR: (*Concerned.*) Where is your husband?

NWANDU: Nne, please, forget that man.

NNEBUOGOR: (*Surprised.*) Forget Onochie?

NWANDU: I thought he was different from the others.

NNEBUOGOR: (*Still concerned.*) Different, how?

NWANDU: Nne, since I moved into that house it's been one quarrel after another.

NNEBUOGOR: (*Shocked.*) Quarrel?

NWANDU: (*Nods vigorously.*) Yes.

NNEBUOGOR: Why do you fight?

NWANDU: He regrets marrying from a family of women. That's

how he puts it.

NNEBUOGOR: (*Unsure.*) Women?

NWANDU: You're a woman. I am a woman. Chizitere is a woman.

NNEBUOGOR: Oh that …

NWANDU: And he didn't know this when he came to ask my hand from a family of women?

NNEBUOGOR: He didn't express any concern about this when he met me or your uncle. In fact, his family praised ours for grooming two lovely women for marriage. They even joked about one of their sons coming to marry Chizitere after you.

NWANDU: So where has all the talk about women come from? This is the question I've asked myself over and over again since I moved into his house. He nags and nags like a woman, while reiterating the fact that I do not have children for him.

NNEBUOGOR: (*Shocked.*) Oh, now it has come to children?

NWANDU: Yes. His mother treats me like her slave, but I've never complained. I wash her clothes, cook all her meals, fetch water for her bath. I do more work than a slave, in fact. Onochie comes with his baggage, too, but he is my husband. I know the challenges that come with marriage that is why I stayed in that house even as I was being maltreated.

NNEBUOGOR: I am surprised that you have returned, because I trained you to remain in your husband's house no matter the circumstance.

NWANDU: I know that, Mama. That is why I even survived up till now.

NNEBUOGOR: Ah ah, I know you can be stubborn sometimes. There's more?

NWANDU: (*Sighs with relief.*) Nne, story for another day.

NNEBUOGOR: You can't say that, Nwandu. What do you expect me to tell your father's brother when he learns that you have returned to your father's house? It is a taboo for a woman to do what you have just done and no one condones that.

NWANDU: I slept outside my husband's house last night, on the steps to his flat. Onochie and his mother practically dragged me out of the house. While I lay there crying with my belongings, they weren't touched. They ignored my tears. They abandoned me there. But for a neighbour who gave me some money this morning to return home, I may have been stranded there.

NNEBUOGOR: (*Consoling her with her left hand.*) Because you have no child yet?

(*Enter* CHIZITERE. *She is surprised to see* NWANDU.*)

CHIZITERE: (*Excited.*) Ah, sister, welcome.

(NWANDU *gets up and they hug briefly.*)

NWANDU: (*Happy.*) How are you doing, my little sister?

CHIZITERE: I am fine. In short, I am excited now that I have seen you.

NWANDU: I hear you will soon become a woman …

CHIZITERE: (*Excitedly.*) Yes oooh, I've always reminded you of how I want to be like you when I grow up. Now I'm grown and I think it's time to be like you.

NWANDU: Do not be in a hurry to say that you want to be like me, my dear sister. Things are not always the way they seem or appear in daylight.

CHIZITERE: But you're happily married. What else is there to see?

NWANDU: There's a lot that you don't know. But sometimes it is even better not to know. You know some people say that a problem you don't know about cannot kill you.

CHIZITERE: Yes, but to be forewarned is to be forearmed.

NWANDU: (*Smiles lightly.*) Yes, people say that, too.

NNEBUOGOR: Zizi, please, help your sister take her bag into her room.

CHIZITERE: (*Looks at the bag and tries to lift it up, surprised.*) Looks like you have come with a lot. Is this going to be a long vacation?

NWANDU: Maybe …

CHIZITERE: What about Onochie? Is he alright?

NNEBUOGOR: (*Cuts in.*) Yes, Chizitere. Onochie is fine. Help your sister take this bag inside first. You have all the time later to talk about Onochie.

CHIZITERE: (*Reluctantly.*) Okay. I hope we'll have plenty of time to talk.

(*She drags the bag offstage. Exit. Lights fade immediately.*)

Scene Four

Lights. NNEBUOGOR's *veranda.* IWEGBU *enters immediately and heads to the door. He starts hitting the door with his walking stick, while calling on* NNEBUOGOR.

IWEGBU: Where is this woman? Nnebuogor! (NNEBUOGOR *enters.*)

NNEBUOGOR: (*Surprised.*) Ah, welcome my husband. I wasn't expecting you.

IWEGBU: (*Uninterested.*) What is this I am hearing, Oriaku?

NNEBUOGOR: (*Interested.*) What did you hear?

IWEGBU: Where is your daughter, Nwandu?

(NNEBUOGOR *is quiet.*)

Because I heard with one ear that she returned to this village with a very big bag, bigger than that which she used to move to her husband's house. Does this not mean that she has abandoned her husband?

NNEBUOGOR: Nna'anyi Iwegbu, please, sit down.

IWEGBU: (*Disappointed.*) Nnebuogor, I do not like the way you and your daughters bring ridicule upon this family. Have I come here to sit because I no longer have chairs to sit at home? Do you think I have come here so you can … In short, go in now and call Nwandu so that I don't lose my temper.

NNEBUOGOR: (*Concerned.*) Nna'anyi, please, sit.

IWEGBU: (*Cuts in, angry.*) Have you lost it, Woman? Go back into this house now and come out with your daughter. I am not in the mood to play.

NNEBUOGOR: Excuse me, Nna'anyi. (*Exit.*)

IWEGBU: (*Talking to the audience.*) Eh heh, how can I ask you to call your daughter only for you to start blabbing? Have I now become your fellow woman?

(*Enter* NNEBUOGOR, NWANDU *and* CHIZITERE.) Sit down, Mrs.

(NNEBUOGOR *sits.* NWANDU *and* CHIZITERE *attempt to join her on the same bench.*)

Tahh! Am I your mate? Are you two not young enough to remain standing?

(*To* NNEBUOGOR.) Woman, you see what I told you earlier. You haven't trained these children properly.

NWANDU: (*Genuflects with* CHIZITERE *at the same time.*) We are sorry, Uncle.

IWEGBU: Chizitere, go and call your uncle, Ezeulu. Quickly.

CHIZITERE: Okay, Uncle. (*Exit.*)

IWEGBU: (*To* NWANDU.) What kind of holiday are you here for? Shouldn't you be in the house of the man who paid your bride price?

NNEBUOGOR: (*To* IWEGBU.) You see, my hus …

IWEGBU: (*Cuts in.*) Shut up, Nnebuogor. Did I ask you to speak?

NNEBUOGOR: No, my husband.

IWEGBU: (*Disappointed.*) Eh heh. Shouldn't you be in your husband's house?

NWANDU: Yes, Uncle. That's exactly where I was until the same man who gave you wine for my head chased me away from my matrimonial home.

IWEGBU: (*Shocked.*) Did you beat his mother or insult any member of his family?

NWANDU: (*Shakes her head in disagreement.*) How can I do such a thing? No.

IWEGBU: Did you steal anything from your husband?

NWANDU: Never!

IWEGBU: Did you fail to cook his food, wash his clothes or manage his manly desires?

NWANDU: I did all those things and even more for my husband.

IWEGBU: And he did not catch you in the arms of another man?

NWANDU: (*Shocked.*) No way. My husband remains the only man who has known my body or touched me. I will never share such privacy with another.

IWEGBU: So why are you here?

(*Enter* EZEULU *and* CHIZITERE. CHIZITERE *returns to her previous position.* EZEULU, *dressed in Igbo chieftaincy regalia, is in his late fifties.*)

EZEULU: Greetings, my brother.

(*Shakes hands with* IWEGBU.)

IWEGBU: Welcome, Ezeulu. Please, sit.

EZEULU: (*Sits. To* NNEBUOGOR.) My in-law, this one all of you are here …

(*To* NWANDU.) You came to visit us?

IWEGBU: (*To* EZEULU.) She is the reason I have asked that you come. She was about to tell us why she has returned to her father's house.

EZEULU: (*Shocked.*) Ah ah …

IWEGBU: Yes. Why have you come back here, Nwandu? I won't ask you again.

NWANDU: (*Sad, but confident.*) Nna'anyi, I haven't known peace since I married that man. That is why I wanted to marry the man I loved but you people said he was *osu*.

IWEGBU: (*Cuts in.*) Shut up! Is that the question I asked?

NWANDU: How can I remain married to a man who cannot perfrom the duties expected of him? Yet, he blames me every day for his misfortunes, he and his mother …

EZEULU: (*Surprised.*) His mother?

NWANDU: Yes.

EZEULU: She's a good woman.

NWANDU: No! She beats me like a child.

EZEULU: Certainly you would have beaten her back.

NWANDU: How can I fight with my husband's mother? I will never do that, Uncle.

IWEGBU: Is that why you left your husband's house? Is it not taboo that you abandoned your husband and all your responsibilities to him as his wife?

EZEULU: A good question, Iwegbu, a good question! Why?

NWANDU: Maybe I should speak explicitly. My husband has rarely touched me since we became man and wife.

(IWEGBU *and* EZEULU *look at each other*).

He reserves his emotions for his sweet mother alone. Yes, he tries to touch me sometimes, only in an attempt to make me pregnant. Yet … He and his mother blame me for not being able to have children. They say I come from a cursed family, one of women and only women.

NNEBUOGOR: (*Cuts in.*) You can imagine.

NWANDU: Yet, the doctor confirmed that Onochie may never father a child without treatment because he suffers from low sperm count.

EZEULU: Chineke!

IWEGBU: So, why blame you?

NWANDU: I am tired, Nna'anyi Iwegbu. His mother has started talking about bringing him a new wife and I am not ready to fight any woman.

NNEBUOGOR: And she thinks that bringing in another wife would take all those problems away?

NWANDU: I don't know. But I am happy for them. When the new wife comes and doesn't get pregnant, then the whole world will know who has the problem.

IWEGBU: (*With mixed feelings.*) Sometimes our ancestors shake things up to work for the good of the family. You are welcome home, my daughter.

(NNEBUOGOR, NWANDU *and* CHIZITERE *are surprised*).

In fact, I am happy now that Emenike's family have all come together under his roof again because we are not happy with the way all of you have handled things since his demise. But that is by the way now. Ezeulu, I think that we can go on and tell them about our decision now that the family is complete.

EZEULU: Please, go ahead, my brother.

IWEGBU: It is the tradition of our people to preserve family lineage no matter what. I was here four days ago, and I told you that Emenike's kinsmen were concerned about the future of his family. Let us call a spade a spade. Nwandu and Chizitere are women and we have considered two options before us traditionally, to ensure that Emenike's name does not just follow him to his grave. First of all, what we want for our late brother is a son – three, two, even one can do. The purpose here is to preserve his lineage. So, two things ... we can all agree to go out there and marry a young woman who would provide this child for us. Many many years ago, it was the duty of the female children of the family to collectively pay the bride price of a younger woman after the demise of their father, so that the new bride could procreate and raise male children to preserve the family lineage. But as we have decided, we may go with this option or ask you, Nwandu, to remain here in your father's house and have children that will preserve his name.

NWANDU: (*Surprised as* NNEBUOGOR *and* CHIZITERE.) Preserve whose name? Are we not talking about me?

EZEULU: It is for the interest of your father that we are seated here now. For the interest of the ...

NWANDU: (*Interrupting him.*) Wait, Sir. Are we not talking about Father? It looks like we have forgotten that I am still married. What about my name?

EZEULU: Didn't you just tell us that you weren't going back to your husband?

IWEGBU: I hope you are not considering going back to that caste boy because that will only happen over my dead body.

NWANDU: I thought the reason we came together this evening was to discuss my problems with my husband. Now, this tradition?

IWEGBU: My daughter, look at this as a way out of your predicament. We can return the bride price we received from Onochie's people, so he doesn't come here tomorrow to call Emenike's children his offspring. Onochie will have no further business here once his money is returned to his people. It is you who would go out there now and identify a well behaved man to make you pregnant. The resulting offspring will belong to the lineage of your father, not to their biological father. If you won't do it, Chizitere will do it.

CHIZITERE: (*Shocked.*) God forbid. I am a Christian. I will not walk in the way of the devil.

IWEGBU: (*Angry.*) Shut up. Are we not your parents? If your mother had not fed you with her breasts would you stand here today to call us non-Christians?

NNEBUOGOR: (*Persuasively.*) My husbands, you know that I've always respected your decisions. I've never disagreed with your views when it comes to matters that concern the family. Please, no matter what we decide to do here, let us leave my daughters out of it. Like you know already, Nwandu is married and Chizitere will soon join her husband in his house once you agree on a date to receive her bride price ...

IWEGBU: (*Cutting in.*) Nnebuogor, don't misunderstand me. I haven't asked your daughters to ignore their marriages or cancel their plans for it. If Emenike was a friend and not a brother, do you think I'll be here? I am not young, so if I've walked all the way from my house to talk to you about a family decision, you should consider it seriously. I don't want us to quarrel about this. Normally, we would take the decision in the absence of your children, but we have called all of you because we also realise that times are changing. You people now go to church. Even Ezeulu has joined you.

NNEBUOGOR: My husbands, you may go ahead and marry a wife for your brother. I will cope with the responsibility of caring for her and her children. You know that I am old too, and I don't want us to make this children suffer for something they know nothing about. Let us make efforts to resolve the problems between Nwandu and Onochie first of all, and then Chizitere and Afamdi's marriage ... That way, we have all the time to search for the bride whom you want to marry for my husband.

EZEULU: (*Coughs.*) Our wife, Nwandu has already told us here that Onochie cannot father a child. So there is no road to that place. It is a no-go area. Unless Nwandu is ready to meet another man who will make her pregnant.

NWANDU: (*Shocked.*) Uncle!

EZEULU: Eh heh! What is wrong with it?

IWEGBU: Nnebuogor, you must caution your children so that they know when to speak in the presence of elders.

NNEBUOGOR: Forgive them, my husband.

IWEGBU: Don't you know Dubem?

NNEBUOGOR: Chimalukem's husband?

IWEGBU: Did he father any one of his children?

NNEBUOGOR: I don't know that one, Nna'anyi Iwegbu.

IWEGBU: It was Dubem's people who suggested that Chima get pregnant by meeting other men because he couldn't make her pregnant.

EZEULU: Is it not better for a woman to get pregnant by another man than for the couple to adopt a strange child from no where?

IWEGBU: At least, the child would have come from one parent.

NWANDU: (*Resisting.*) Uncle, I cannot bring myself to do that. No!

NNEBUOGOR: Nwandu, please, keep quiet.

EZEULU: No. Let her talk. Let her tell us how she intends to settle the dispute in her household. Perhaps, she has a better plan.

NWANDU: (*Looks away.*) Uncle, I will not return to Onochie and his people. So, yes, no-go area. But I will not do anything with another man who will not pay my bride price. I'm not a prostitute.

(*To* NNEBUOGOR.) And, Mama, no woman, whether young or old, is coming into this house. If Uncle wants to marry for Papa, they can do so on their own, no problem. But the new wife should live with them. She should remain there in their houses.

IWEGBU: Nnebuogor, is your daughter talking to us? Are you hearing her? (*Turns face from all of them.*)

NNEBUOGOR: My in-law, what else do you want me to do? I can only ask her to keep quiet. I cannot get a cane to flog her if she doesn't. She is no longer a child.

EZEULU: (*To* IWEGBU.) My brother, are you listening?

NWANDU: Uncle, nobody has asked you not to carry on with your plans o! But do so and manage the consequences yourself. We've been quiet because we respect you. But you will not impose any more burdens on us.

CHIZITERE: (*Nodding.*) Yes, Uncle.

EZEULU: (*Angry.*) Shut up! Because we let your big sister talk? Are your thinking faculties intact?

(*To* IWEGBU.) Brother, I think we should leave now. We have delivered our decision to them. Nobody has asked them to like it. They don't have to. We are bringing Emenike's wife here and we do not need his children's approval to do so. Nnebuogor has already asked us to go ahead. Isn't it, Oriaku?

NNEBUOGOR: (*Indifferent.*) My in-law, I cannot object to your decisions.

NWANDU: (*Surprised.*) Mama!

EZEULU: (*Cuts in.*) Shut up! Didn't your Bible teach you not to disobey your elders?

NWANDU: Uncle, the Bible does not also agree with the imposition of a second wife on a dead man.

EZEULU: (*Angry.*) I said shut up!

NNEBUOGOR: Please, Nwandu. That is enough.

EZEULU: I was born long before you and I received the Bible before you started reading it. Don't tell me what it says and what it doesn't. You should respect your elders at all times if you want your days to be long.

IWEGBU: (*Sharply.*) Ezeulu! Let us go.

NNEBUOGOR: (*To* IWEGBU.) Please, my in-laws, I hope we haven't struck the wrong cord.

IWEGBU: Let us go, Ezeulu. (*Both men rise and exit.*)

NWANDU: (*Goes to sit on the chair. CHIZITERE joins her.*) You cannot be calm and soft with these men, Mama. How can they openly ask us to sleep around? For God's sake, have we become that cheap? Shouldn't these men be our uncles? How can they come up with such ungodly suggestions?

CHIZITERE: And Mama nodded with them.

NNEBUOGOR: No! I cannot stop them from bringing in another woman for their brother, but they should leave both of you out of it. That's all I'm concerned about. Patience is the mother of a beautiful child. To run is not necessarily to arrive. You will be patient with your uncles. I cannot tell what they can or can't do. We should follow them small small. *Biko nu.*

NWANDU: No, Mama. They have no right to bring in a new wife for Papa. He is our father. They are his brothers. There is a huge difference.

(*Disgusted.*) What are we talking about here? Is Papa not dead anymore?

(*Lights fade quickly.*)

Scene Five

Days after. At NNEBUOGOR's *compound.* IWEGBU *enters with* VALERIA, *a beautiful young lady in her twenties, who trails slowly behind him. She carries a small bag in her right hand.* IWEGBU *goes straight to hit the door with his cane.*

IWEGBU: (*Calling.*) Nnebuogor!

NNEBUOGOR: Nna'anyi.

> (*Enters in the company of* NWANDU *and* ULAEVUCHI. *They exchange greetings while* VALERIA *remains quiet.*) Welcome, my husband.

IWEGBU: (*Signalling with his hand for* VALERIA *to come forward.*) This is your new wife. Emenike settled her bride price this afternoon.

> (NWANDU *and* ULAEVUCHI *look at* VALERIA *angrily.*)

NNEBUOGOR: (*Surprised.*) Oh! My in-law has kept his word.

IWEGBU: Yes. You will take her inside. Show her to her room. You mustn't forget to provide food and ensure that she has a warm bath. She's a new wife. We don't want to make her run away.

NNEBUOGOR: No, my in-law. She is welcome.

IWEGBU: Take her inside.

NWANDU: (*Angry.*) Take her to where, Mama?

NNEBUOGOR: Nwandu, please. (*To* VALERIA.) Come, my dear. What do they call you?

VALERIA: (*Moving closer to* NNEBUOGOR. *She talks slowly.*) Valeria.

NWANDU: Mama, you people will not tempt me this afternoon o!

ULAEVUCHI: (*Supporting* NWANDU.) Eh heh! That's the spirit.

Speak softly and carry a big stick, you will go far.

NWANDU: She can go with Uncle and live with him. But to stay in this house, I will not be part of this demonic arrangement. He married her, so he should keep her in his house.

NNEBUOGOR: Nwandu, please, don't make trouble in front of your uncle. Let us be patient.

IWEGBU: I was wondering why you cannot control your daughter. Take Valeria inside. She must be hungry by now.

(NWANDU *and* ULAEVUCH *physically block* NNEBUOGOR *and* VALERIA *from going into the house.*)

NNEBUOGOR: Please, Ula, the river may be wide but we will cross it. Take Nwandu inside and talk to her.

ULAEVUCHI: Ogor, I'm sorry o! Let this be the one thing I'll do for you. This girl will come into this house over my dead body.

IWEGBU: (*Angry.*) Will you get out of there, you evil woman?

ULAEVUCHI: Oh! I am evil, and you are not? A good man, I'm sure. Yet, you have brought another woman for your late brother. Since you like her very much to stand here and shout, what is preventing you from taking her home to your wife? She can also bathe her and give her food to eat.

IWEGBU: Nnebuogor, did you bring this nuisance here to wash her dirty linen? The same woman has pushed her husband to drinking with her tongue. I know how dirty your mouth is. What else can your desolate brain conjure?

(*To* NNEBUOGOR.) You don't have to turn around and look at every dog that barks at you. Here is Emenike's wife, you know what is expected of you. I have done my bit. I am going.

ULAEVUCHI: (*Sarcastic.*) Just like that? Have you finished talking?

NNEBUOGOR: Leave him alone, Ulaevuchi. Please, go, Nna'anyi Iwegbu.

NWANDU: (*Moves to block exit.*) No, Mama. Uncle is not going anywhere without his new wife.

IWEGBU: (*Surprised.*) Goodness me! When did this young woman grow so big to challenge me? Have you no fear in you? You see what I tell you always, you have spoiled these children beyond repair. If not, how can a girl who isn't up to the age of my last child stand before me and talk like this?

NNEBUOGOR: (*Apologetic.*) I am very sorry, my husband.

IWEGBU: No! What are you sorry for? That she stands before me to insult my grey hair or for your inability to bring her up well?

ULAEVUCHI: Please, shut up, old man!

NNEBUOGOR: (*Surprised at* ULAEVUCHI.) Jesus Christ, Ula! How can you talk to my in-law in that manner?

ULAEVUCHI: (*To* NNEBUOGOR.) You were not here when he addressed me in a similar tone? He called my brain desolate. But his isn't?

(*To* IWEGBU.) What kind of man are you?

(*Recollecting.*) I pushed my husband to drinking. You are not afraid to say such nonsense before me. There is no way that you'll leave this compound without this harlot you married for your brother.

NNEBUOGOR: (*Stopping* ULAEVUCHI.) Please, no more. No more, I beg you.

ULAEVUCHI: No, no, no, Nne. Let Iwegbu and his kinsmen take her away. They can all draw up a timetable for themselves so that they can each make her pregnant. One who causes others misfortune also teaches them wisdom.

IWEGBU: You see what I'm saying? Sure enough, show me your friend and I will tell you exactly who you are.

NWANDU: (*Disgusted.*) Please, don't come here with that sermon, Uncle. Shouldn't it apply to you as well? If you must marry a wife for my father, then she should be buried with him.

VALERIA: (*Reluctantly.*) No o!

NWANDU: Eh heh, isn't she his wife?

ULAEVUCHI: We can call the youths to dig up Emenike's grave and then she can join him there.

NWANDU: That is the only way this girl can live in this compound. If not in that grave, then she must go back with you or return to wherever she came from.

IWEGBU: All of you are mad.

ULAEVUCHI: It is you who is mad. Take your mistress along with you. Unless you're ready, we will all stand out here. Nobody will tell you when your legs become weak.

VALERIA: (*Recoils.*) Nna'anyi Iwegbu, please, I don't want to cause any problem.

IWEGBU: Shut up, Valeria. This is your husband's house.

ULAEVUCHI: (*Pointing at Emenike's grave.*) There's her husband's house.

IWEGBU: You people are really mad. I am going to my house. If you like, strip yourselves naked. I have fulfilled my obligation as Emenike's brother.

(*To* NWANDU.) Leave that door, my friend.

(*Walks towards her.*)

NWANDU: Uncle, I'm not sure you understand what I said earlier. It is either you take this girl along with you or she stays there in Papa's grave. (*Pointing at Emenike's grave.*)

IWEGBU: Eh heh, go and put her in the grave. What else can I do beyond what I've already done?

NWANDU: You will put her in the grave yourself, Uncle. We aren't going to do that for you. (*Sarcastically.*) You are the man here and the head of the family.

(NNEBUOGOR *is tired of the whole episode, goes to sit.*)

IWEGBU: Oh! This is what you people learn nowadays in the Church?

NWANDU: No. One man, one wife. It's there in the Bible.

IWEGBU: (*Laughing awkwardly.*) It is there in the Bible. May Amadioha strike this head of yours.

ULAEVUCHI: (*Moves to join* NWANDU.) It is your head that Amadioha will strike.

IWEGBU: Nnebuogor, you are just sitting there. By the time I report your daughter to my kinsmen, you people will have nowhere to run. Ask them to leave this door now, let me go to my house. Ears that do not listen to advice, accompany the head when it is chopped.

ULAEVUCHI: (*Laughing.*) You can't face a woman then. Come and pass let me see. Head of the family, my foot. It is old men like you who go about fomenting trouble when it is uncalled for. Did Emenike ask you to marry a wife for him? You have fulfilled your duties as the firstborn. Go and marry your harlot so that you can expand your lineage. My sister is not interested in expanding hers.

(*There's a knock on the door. They all keep quiet and pretend not to hear it until it happens again.*)

NWANDU: (*Shouting.*) Who?

CHIZITERE: (*From backstage.*) Me, Sister.

NWANDU: (*Opening the door.*) Come in quickly.

(*While* CHIZITERE *comes in,* IWEGBU *tries to exit forcefully through a narrow exit.* NWANDU *and* ULAEVUCHI *make attempts to prevent him from exiting.)*

IWEGBU: (*Struggling to exit.*) Idiots! (*Exit.*)

CHIZITERE: (*Curious, VALERIA backs her.*) Sister, what is happening?

(*To* ULAEVUCHI.) Good afternoon, Aunty.

NWANDU: (*Regretfully.*) We shouldn't have opened that door.

CHIZITERE: (*To* ULAEVUCHI.) Aunty?

ULAEVUCHI: Your uncle has deposited your father's second wife here for your mother.

CHIZITERE: (*Shocked and angry.*) What, Uncle went on to do that?

NWANDU: (*Pointing at* VALERIA.) See for yourself …

CHIZITERE: (*Moving closer to* VALERIA, *surprised to see her.*) Valeria! (*All are surprised.* VALERIA *turns away.*)

NNEBUOGOR: You know her?

CHIZITERE: Yes. We are in the choir together.

NWANDU: (*Surprised, to* VALERIA.) You're a Christian? (VALERIA *is quiet.*) And you agreed to this fetish marriage?

ULAEVUCHI: (*Laughs briefly.*) You see. All of you jumped into the Christian ship in a hurry. Now see, your fellow churchgoer. She now wants to marry the dead.

CHIZITERE: (*Unhappy.*) Valeria, what are you doing here?

(NNEBUOGOR *rises and exits.* NWANDU *and* ULAEVUCHI *angrily join her.*)

VALERIA: (*Turning to her.*) I don't want to cause any problems for your family, please.

CHIZITERE: (*Shouting.*) Oh, then, what are you doing here in my father's house?

VALERIA: We don't have to shout down the roof of your house.

Mazi Iwegbu and his kinsmen came to my father's house and told him that they wanted to marry me and my bride price was agreed and settled. That's the short of the story. That's why I am here in my husband's house.

CHIZITERE: You don't know that my father died years ago?

VALERIA: We've discussed all the details and it's not a problem for me.

CHIZITERE: I thought you are a Christian. How can you do this?

VALERIA: (*Unconcerned.*) Well, Father says it may be my destiny. My trespasses are the gods' will and Mazi's wish. They have already ordained me to be Emenike's wife.

CHIZITERE: (*Disgusted.*) What gods? Were you pretending in the Church? Don't you know what the Bible says about things like this?

VALERIA: Why should I? Let us not go there at all. We all know that the Bible is not for us but for the Israelites.

(*Sarcastically.*) Thou shall not have any other god before me … Nonsense. Father says the first commandment of God in the Bible does not apply to us. The early Christian missionaries were mainly Europeans who didn't bother to learn about our gods and goddesses. They just jumped into making conclusions of their own and we swallowed everything they told us. Our deities do not disagree on the existence of a God in heaven. So, why should Christianity confront them in this manner? No one can reconcile with the king if he doesn't first do so with the king's agents that he has offended. God was and is still here with us as he was and is with the people of Israel and Eurasia. Yes, Father said that. Your cathechist was in my house to see my father last week and Father asked him a pertinent question. Jude was canonised a saint because the invocation of his name cured a patient in India. Yet, have we tried in our moments of distress to invoke the names of our departed to see if we could get the help we need? Cathechist was numb. I don't see anything wrong with being Catholic and observing some aspects of my tradition at the same time.

CHIZITERE: (*Unhappy.*) In other words, you are staying?

VALERIA: This is my husband's house. I have no place else to go.

CHIZITERE: I was foolish to think that we were friends. How can you agree to do this to me and my family?

(VALERIA *is silent.*)

You didn't know Mazi Emenike was my father? It is only a stupid cow that rejoices at the prospect of being taken to a beautiful abattoir.

VALERIA: My dear Chizitere, it is already too late to go in search of excuses that will make me run away. I was well informed of the arrangement and they also told me about the challenges that would come from my husband's family.

CHIZITERE: And you are prepared to face them?

VALERIA: Isn't it obvious already?

CHIZITERE: He who eats another man's food will have his own food eaten by others.

VALERIA: Until then …

CHIZITERE: (*Smiles sarcastically.*) You are here to stay.

(*Lights fade quickly.*)

Scene Six

Lights. ONWUAMAIBE's *living room. He is eating akpu with bitter leaf soup from two plates, a flat one and a bowl. Enter* ULAEVUCHI *with a bowl of water and a towel.*

ULAEVUCHI: Ibe'm, water to wash your hands. (*Presents bowl to* ONWUAMAIBE).

ONWUAMAIBE: Thank you, Ula. (*Washing both hands. After five seconds, he takes a towel and cleans his hands.*) Thank you. Chewing stick?

ULAEVUCHI: Here.

(*Hands him one from the table. Immediately, she takes his plates and water and exits stage. She returns after a minute and joins* ONWUAMAIBE *to sit.*)

ONWUAMAIBE: Iwegbu reported you to the elders' council. Says you insulted him, or should I say you harassed him?

ULAEVUCHI: (*Undisturbed.*) Okay. He expects them to flog me? Would he feel better to harass me back?

ONWUAMAIBE: You don't always have to go looking for trouble, especially when the bone of contention doesn't involve you.

ULAEVUCHI: When it does?

ONWUAMAIBE: Well, I don't know. I can't always beg those you offend. Your cup gets full and you're on your own.

ULAEVUCHI: You can't cut me some slack. I must always be the one who is wrong.

ONWUAMAIBE: I didn't say that.

ULAEVUCHI: Yes. But they come to you and you apologise before hearing my side.

ONWUAMAIBE: (*Cuts in.*) Because I know you. You're like a

magnet for trouble.

ULAEVUCHI: I don't blame you. Even so, I am your wife. If you do not stand by me and defend me, who will?

ONWUAMAIBE: Well, I'm not very keen to know why you go about making trouble. But I'll advise you to desist from it. One day *monkey go go market and e no go return*.

ULAEVUCHI: Please, go and tell that to Iwegbu who forcefully imposed a young girl on my friend.

ONWUAMAIBE: How does that concern you, Ula?

ULAEVUCHI: Nnebuogor is my friend. We are like five and six.

ONWUAMAIBE: So what? She's not your sister!

ULAEVUCHI: You know how soft she can be and you want me to sit back and watch somebody like Iwegbu and his kinsmen maltreat her?

ONWUAMAIBE: No one is maltreating Nnebuogor. You talk like I don't know her myself. She is a wise woman. If she wants to accept the other woman in her husband's house, then let her do so. She knows the right thing to do. You shouldn't dabble into matters of tradition in haste, else it consumes you. Please, allow Nnebuogor and her family to manage their crisis on their own. Let us mind our business so that others won't do so for us.

ULAEVUCHI: Okay o! I won't take such embarrassment from anyone, even if it is your kinsmen. Just so you know.

ONWUAMAIBE: I know you. Didn't I say that before?

(*Lights fade.*)

Scene Seven

After two days. Lights. VALERIA *is seated in front of* NNEBUOGOR'*s house. She has obviously settled in. Beside her is a short stool on which are placed a small bag, a mirror and some cosmetics.* VALERIA *picks the mirror and starts admiring her face; she touches her hair now and then, and rises.*

VALERIA: (*Using the mirror to look at her body.*) Who says that I am not beautiful? Let him go and jump into the Idemili River.

(*After a moment, she sits back down and starts applying make-up to her face while miming to a local Christian song.*)

(*Enter* CHIZITERE.)

CHIZITERE: (*Yawns.*) Good morning.

VALERIA: Eh heh, good morning, Chizitere.

CHIZITERE: You're up early.

VALERIA: (*Continuing with her make-up.*) Yes.

CHIZITERE: You woke up the same way yesterday and you were gone for the whole day.

VALERIA: Yes.

CHIZITERE: You're going out again today?

VALERIA: Yes, many errands to run.

CHIZITERE: May I ask where?

VALERIA: I don't think this is any of your business.

CHIZITERE: You're in my father's house so it's all my business.

VALERIA: Am I not supposed to get pregnant for your father? You think I will get pregnant by sitting here at home and watching the sun rise and set? Hmn, you have a lot to learn.

CHIZITERE: You disgust me.

VALERIA: I do?

CHIZITERE: You're not even ashamed to tell the world that you sleep around?

VALERIA: I thought you asked where I was going. Besides, what's there to be ashamed of? Your mother didn't do it?

CHIZITERE: How dare you bring my mother into this?

VALERIA: (*Unperturbed.*) Please … you are no saint, all of you. We all have skeletons in our drawers. If you don't mind, I have to look beautiful to catch the best bird out there. Times are tough.

CHIZITERE: God forgive you.

VALERIA: Have I lied? Every living thing can attest to my beauty. Even the birds, you can hear them, they are singing it. No wonder Mazi Iwegbu chose me. One who plants grapes by the roadside, and one who marries a beautiful woman share the same problem.

CHIZITERE: And you think it's enough to be beautiful? Too much of it with no good character is worse than being ugly. Isn't the surface of the water beautiful? Yet, it is no good to sleep on.

VALERIA: Do I smell jealousy in the tone of your voice?

CHIZITERE: What you smell, Mrs, is the truth and yes, it is bitter.

VALERIA: (*Drops mirror, laughing loudly.*) I must warn you, step-daughter, let not my beauty confuse you. I am not very kind like your mother and I cannot always be patient. The moon, the sun and the stars may be beautiful, but the sky also has a threatening thunder and striking lightning.

CHIZITERE: Are you saying that to scare me?

VALERIA: I am not a crow. I don't scare. I am beautiful, I draw people to me.

CHIZITERE: You make me laugh. Of what use is the beauty of a woman if there's no one to admire it?

VALERIA: No one? You are the one who is funny, I tell you. My husband may be dead, but that doesn't stop others from admiring me.

CHIZITERE: In all your heart, you are convinced men will meet with a dead man's wife? They'll be too afraid to even touch you.

VALERIA: (*Smiles.*) I told you. You are comedy. This is my third day in this house and I can assure you I've had more fun in these few days than all the fun your mother has had in her lifetime.

CHIZITERE: May God forgive you. May our Mother Mary and the Angels and Saints in heaven pray for you. Your soul is already doomed.

VALERIA: And you are the judge of the doomed souls. (*Laughing.*)

CHIZITERE: (*Shakes her head in pity.*) Really, I pity you.

VALERIA: I shouldn't be making this conversation with my step-daughter. Get me something to eat, now!

CHIZITERE: (*Laughs.*) Valeria, you've obviously lost bearing. Are you mad already?

VALERIA: And you, my dear, shall not speak to me in that manner, unless you want your kinsmen to settle us.

CHIZITERE: What stops you from calling them?

VALERIA: You can be banished if you fail to shut up now and accord me the respect I deserve.

CHIZITERE: You earn respect, not buy it. For your information, you do not give the orders here.

VALERIA: (*Laughs.*) I can do whatever I want. I am the new wife. This is my husband's house.

CHIZITERE: You're so sick and disgusting. Where have all your morals gone? (*Angrily exits stage.*)

VALERIA: (*Speaking to the audience.*) They had better realise that I'm here to stay. I'm not going anywhere.

(*Suddenly takes a bag and puts all her cosmetics and the mirror in it. Rises, looks around the compound and exits through the left downstage entrance.*)

(*Enter NWANDU in a hurry. CHIZITERE is behind her.*)

NWANDU: (*Looking around.*) Where's she? I thought you said she was here now?

CHIZITERE: She must have gone out already.

NWANDU: (*Uses her fist to hit her other palm.*) Her *chi* is definitely with her this morning.

(*Obviously angry.*) It is Mama that is causing all this. For how long should we swallow whatever they shove down our throats? Me, I am not going to live with you people in this house.

CHIZITERE: You will go back to Onochie?

NWANDU: Who said anything about him?

CHIZITERE: Oh.

NWANDU: Onochie is my past. I won't go back to it.

CHIZITERE: So?

NWANDU: (*In a hushed tone.*) Ogbo. He is my first love.

CHIZITERE: And they said you can't marry from his family.

NWANDU: Who are they? They can't impose a second wife on Papa and expect that I'll let them choose who I marry or not. Didn't I go along with their decision in the first place? Look where it landed me …

CHIZITERE: Well, Onochie was your friend, too.

NWANDU: And Valeria isn't your friend? A close friend can become a close enemy.

CHIZITERE: That one, she is like a pretty road, but crooked. I really thought that she was my friend. If someone warned me, I'd say that Valeria isn't the kind, now look.

NWANDU: Yes. Dogs do not actually prefer bones to meat, it is just that no one ever gives them meat.

CHIZITERE: She has stopped coming to choir practice.

NWANDU: I'd be surprised if she's even admitted into the Church for anything. How can such a person face God?

CHIZITERE: Eventually, she's the one the Church was established for. Jesus called sinners to repent and come to him. Maybe we should pray for her.

NWANDU: (*Irritated.*) And you're beginning to sound like Mama.

CHIZITERE: I'm beginning to think that she has a point.

NWANDU: You people are drunk in this house. No wonder Uncle takes us for granted. How long was I away? This house has fallen already. Oh, how I miss Papa. I will not tolerate any form of imposition on me from Papa's family. Valeria will never be welcome here. If you and Mama want to take care of her, then it's okay. You will do that alone. She can serve as my replacement because I'll be gone before anyone notices.

(*Enter* NNEBUOGOR.)

CHIZITERE: Good morning, Mama.

NNEBUOGOR: Good morning, Zizi. Has Valeria gone out already? She's not inside.

CHIZITERE: She has gone out to get pregnant.

NNEBUOGOR: That's what she's supposed to do. (*Goes to sit.*)

CHIZITERE: (*Surprised.*) Hmm, she should be careful o! The scourge is still spreading here and there.

NWANDU: Maybe becoming Christians is not such a good thing. How can you support such a tradition and still be a Christian?

NNEBUOGOR: Stop there. We cannot because of our new religion not offer kola or pour libations to our ancestors. Even Jesus told us to give to Caesar and give to God. We will not throw out the baby with the bath water. I did not bring you up to go around making trouble. Your father's kinsmen took this decision in your father's interest.

NWANDU: (*Cuts in.*) Lies, Mama. How is this in Papa's interest? You are too old to start telling lies, Mama.

NNEBUOGOR: And you are too young to understand that some times we must let our guards down and allow elders take decisions on our behalf.

NWANDU: (*Cutting in.*) You're wrong, Mama. We cannot allow elders take decisions that they won't live with. Was it my decision to marry Onochie? Uncle Ezeulu hand-picked him as my husband because his mother is his friend. Did he come around to stop them from beating me? He didn't take a pinch of the suffering they made me go through. I should have gone along with the man who first stole my heart.

NNEBUOGOR: Please, don't say that again. We didn't call Ogbonnaya a bad man. But we told you why you couldn't marry him. That subject is closed and we will not go back to it.

NWANDU: (*Quietly.*) Let us hope so, Mama, because I'm tired of doing this already.

(*Enter* VALERIA. *She walks up to* NNEBUOGOR. NWANDU *looks away from her.*)

VALERIA: Nne, good morning.

NNEBUOGOR: My daughter, how are you?

VALERIA: (*Smiles.*) I am okay. Thank you. Can I join you?

NNEBUOGOR: Please, feel free. This is your house, too.

VALERIA: (*Joining* NNEBUOGOR *on the bench.*) Thank you.

NNEBUOGOR: Did you eat your morning food before going
out?

VALERIA: They didn't give me food o! I told Chizitere. Ask her.

NNEBUOGOR: Chizitere, please, go inside and get her morning
food.

(CHIZITERE *looks at* VALERIA *badly for five seconds and
exits angrily.* NWANDU *follows in the same manner. Lights
fade slowly.*)

Scene Eight

Lights. In front of IWEGBU's *house. He enters, dressed in full Igbo chieftaincy attire. He is on his way out. Enter* Mazi EZEULU *from the left downstage entrance. He meets* IWEGBU *locking his door.*

EZEULU: My brother, looks like you are going out.

IWEGBU: (*Turning to* EZEULU.) Yes. I have a meeting at the Igwe's palace.

EZEULU: Your family? They must have gone out.

IWEGBU: They have all gone to the church.

EZEULU: Oh oh, everybody is already turning a new leaf.

IWEGBU: And I will not object yet, until it gets in my way. Then, we'll know who heads the home.

EZEULU: Christianity brings its own advantages. The flavour of it differs from our traditional religion.

IWEGBU: You're now sounding like a woman. They are the target of the Church. Through them the Church gets to us.

EZEULU: I'm not even trying to bring you into it because I'm still trying to find my footing in it. But it is extraordinary, the new religion. Jesus Christ calls you unto his bosom and he offers salvation for free, without bias or traditional consecration. Yet, he taketh away the sins of man without punishment.

IWEGBU: No more, Ezeulu. I'm not interested in departing from that which we've been doing from countless ages back. Your religion is good, but it will not buy me over by warning of the dangers of hell and depicting the joys of heaven. At least, we agree on the existence of one Supreme God, his goodness, and so on. That one is enough for me.

EZEULU: (*Smiles.*) Okay o! You hear what Emenike's widow is doing for his new bride. She's getting used to it.

IWEGBU: I told you. She will, the others, too. They do not have a choice.

EZEULU: Yes. And the small girl, she's still mounting pressure on me to talk to you so that Afamdi's people can come and see us.

IWEGBU: I thought we've dropped that boy's issue for now.

EZEULU: We have.

IWEGBU: Let Valeria get pregnant first, then we'll know what to do with Chizitere and the young man. We cannot use our hands to tie a rope around our neck, lest we suffocate and block food from going through our throat.

EZEULU: That is true.

IWEGBU: (*Using his cane to gesticulate.*) Are you going back home or that way?

EZEULU: Let me go back.

IWEGBU: Okay.

(IWEGBU *and* EZEULU *walk offstage as lights fade slowly.*)

Scene Nine

Lights. NNEBUOGOR's *front yard.* ONOCHIE *and* NWANDU *burst out of the house unto the stage arguing.*

NWANDU: You and your mother, there is nothing you will do in this life to take me back to that house.

ONOCHIE: Why would you say such a thing? I am still your husband and I want us to return together.

NWANDU: Onochie, no!

ONOCHIE: I still love you, Nwandu. I've not had a complete day of happiness since you left.

NWANDU: Was I happy myself when I lived with you and your mother?

ONOCHIE: Please, my wife …

NWANDU: (*Cuts in.*) Mama is your wife.

ONOCHIE: Don't say that Mama is my wife. I am ready to change, Mama, too.

NWANDU: Too late, ex-husband! You had your chance and you lost it.

ONOCHIE: No, I haven't.

NWANDU: (*Smiles.*) Oh, yes, you have. Check again. My family will come and meet your people soon to return my bride price.

ONOCHIE: My people will not accept.

NWANDU: They had better. I will not be forced again to engage in a transaction that wouldn't guarantee my joy.

ONOCHIE: I have spoken to Mama. She has changed, I promise you.

NWANDU: You?

ONOCHIE: I wouldn't have come if I was still the same old Onochie. Please, forgive me.

NWANDU: (*Emotional.*) Onochie, your mother beat me. She treated me like a slave. No human deserves such treatment from anybody, no matter what.

ONOCHIE: She won't do that again. I promise.

NWANDU: Why doesn't she come here to make the promise herself?

ONOCHIE: She told me. She sends her apologies.

NWANDU: She's too proud, of course.

ONOCHIE: No, she isn't.

NWANDU: Well, I've made myself very clear. Nothing will take me back to your house. Where I'm from, when we say a thing is over, it is.

ONOCHIE: Nwandu, you can't forget the good times because of a few days of misunderstanding.

NWANDU: Is that what it was to you? Your mother put me in hell. She threw me out of your house to sleep outside and you call that a few days of misunderstanding? Maybe you should leave now.

ONOCHIE: Please, my wife, I am sorry. Anything, just ask. I will do whatever it takes to get us back together as man and wife.

NWANDU: Are you certain that you'd do anything?

ONOCHIE: Yes, *omalicha'm.*

NWANDU: Okay. Here's what you should do.

ONOCHIE: (*Zealous.*) What?

NWANDU: Take that machete and slice your throat, that way you'd die. I'll mourn you for six months and move on with my life. It is so much sweeter without you in it.

ONOCHIE: Has it gotten so bad that you wish me dead?

NWANDU: Death cannot be bad enough for you and Mama. Maybe something worse should swallow you two alive so that you can feel the pain and misery both of you put me through.

ONOCHIE: I wouldn't have imagined that you were this angry and hurt, my wife.

NWANDU: No, you wouldn't, because if you did, you would have stopped your mother. But you listened to her. She's your alpha and omega, your beginning and your end. As for me and my family, we've washed all of you off our lives. No member of my family is willing to step foot in your village again. Our bond died that night you threw me out in the cold. My spirit left yours and it has loitered since then in search of love again.

ONOCHIE: You mustn't love another man.

NWANDU: Says who?

ONOCHIE: Me! I am your husband.

NWANDU: (*Laughs.*) You're very funny, Onochie. A husband's love is no child's play. You don't profess it and not show it. You don't love me. Mama is the one you love and I will not fight to get in between you two. I'm no heartbreaker.

ONOCHIE: (*Kneels on one knee before* NWANDU.) Come with me, Nwandu. I will make you the happiest woman in the world.

NWANDU: Didn't you say that before? You've lost your chance to make me happy. I won't be deceived again by your calm and deceitful apology. Go home and tell that to your mother.

ONOCHIE: Live with me again for one week, just one week. If you notice for a second that I am no changed man, you may pack your bags and leave. And I promise, I will ask my people to come to yours to request for and collect your bride price. After which, you will never see me again.

NWANDU: What about children?

ONOCHIE: (*Rising.*) That ... (*Backs* NWANDU.)

NWANDU: Yes, that. That was the basis of our problems, wasn't it? Your mother called me barren for as long as we saw each other, true or false?

ONOCHIE: True.

NWANDU: They blamed me for our childlessness. You didn't tell them that ...

ONOCHIE: (*Cuts in, turning to* NWANDU.) Let's not go there again, please.

NWANDU: Why?

ONOCHIE: I have informed my kinsmen. They know why we do not have children. But ...

NWANDU: (*Cuts in.*) What?

ONOCHIE: We have agreed to permit you to go outside and meet with any man you choose to make you pregnant.

NWANDU: (*Disgusted and angry.*) What!

ONOCHIE: Please, don't shout.

NWANDU: All of you have gone mad! How dare you? You and your kinsmen must have no iota of respect for womanhood. You must also think that I am a slut. I will do no such thing, Onochie. Go back to your kinsmen and tell them that you have lost me. They should accompany you to get a new wife. Period!

ONOCHIE: Please, let us not shout and make these things public. We do this quietly, we live happily ever after. No one gets hurt. I am not the first man who would ask his wife to do this. I definitely won't be the last.

NWANDU: I will never accede to such nonsense. Even if I am mad and I agree, what makes me different from my father's brothers? I won't join in this madness. I am beginning to suspect that a contagious bug is moving around and catching up with you people. If not, why will your people act in the same way as my uncles? I won't bend. I'd rather return to my first love or die a single woman.

ONOCHIE: No, you won't die a single woman and you won't marry another man.

NWANDU: But another man can make me pregnant? (*Angry.*) Please, get out of my house, Onochie. I've been patient enough.

ONOCHIE: I won't leave until you agree to go with me.

NWANDU: Okay then. You can stay here. I'm off to see my friends. (*Exit.*)

ONOCHIE: (*Going to sit on the bench.*) I will wait, even if I have to sleep here.

(*After a moment,* VALERIA *enters wearing a waist wrapper and a resembling one which covers her breasts. Her navel and shoulders are completely bare. She walks slowly to* ONOCHIE, *who sits worriedly, and joins him on the bench.*)

VALERIA: You are unhappy. What is the trouble?

(ONOCHIE *is quiet.*) What has put you in this mood?

ONOCHIE: My wife. She's impossible.

VALERIA: Oh. You know that, too. I was beginning to wonder if I was alone in thinking that. She's giving you a tough time, I presume.

ONOCHIE: I've wronged her, I know. At the same time, I've apologised.

VALERIA: Don't worry. Nwandu is a difficult person most of the time. She'll come out of the robe soon. Don't give yourself a headache over her.

ONOCHIE: I just want her back.

VALERIA: (*Changing the subject.*) You came all the way from your village. Did she give you food?

ONOCHIE: No. (*Sighs.*)

VALERIA: She is very difficult, I tell you. Always harsh, even to her husband. Please, don't show her that you want her back so badly. She'll come along.

(*Places her right hand on* ONOCHIE*'s shoulder.*) Come, let me make you some food to eat. Then, you can stay inside and wait for her to return. Please …

(VALERIA *rises and takes* ONOCHIE *by the hand. He rises, too, and they enter the house together. Lights fade.*)

Scene Ten

Three months gone. Lights reveal NNEBUOGOR's front yard. Just like in scene three, she is sitting on a bamboo stool, sifting chaff from a bowl of rice. She sits quietly, concentrating on the chore. Enter NWANDU and ONOCHIE briskly from the main exit, downstage left. They move centre stage and start arguing.

NWANDU: Why won't you let me be, Onochie?

ONOCHIE: What more do you want? I have suffered enough, don't you think?

NWANDU: You should suffer more, lest you fail to learn how to treat a woman.

(NNEBUOGOR *pretends not to be interested in their conversation. She rises and exits into the house with her bowl.*)

ONOCHIE: The Nwandu I married was kinder. What has gotten to you?

NWANDU: Hatred for you and your mother. Hatred for the day I first set my eyes on you. Hatred for the day I moved into your house. You don't deserve a moment of my time.

ONOCHIE: Can we behave like adults? We don't want to upset Mama.

NWANDU: You think I'm worried about my mother? She knows my stand in all this. She will not meddle in my affairs. Please, go home.

ONOCHIE: (*Belches, talking to himself.*) Love is a despot. It spares no one.

NWANDU: (*Unimpressed.*) And yes, like coffee, it tastes best when hot.

ONOCHIE: Can you no longer feel something for me?

NWANDU: (*Laughs.*) Is that a question? If it is, I answered a long time ago. My heart no longer has reservation for you.

ONOCHIE: Just another chance. You don't have to love me back. We can grow in love again. Let me show you the new man in me.

NWANDU: Onochie, I'm not interested in the man in you. I will never return to you and your wicked kinsmen whom you've plotted with to turn me into their sleeping mattress.

ONOCHIE: No. You don't have to go out anymore to meet another.

NWANDU: (*Surprised, curious.*) Because?

ONOCHIE: (*Moves face away a little.*) Go and look at Valeria.

NWANDU: (*Curious.*) What happened to her?

ONOCHIE: You live together in this house and you don't know?

NWANDU: (*Considering the message.*) Know what? (*Suddenly remembers, clutches her head.*) Christ! (*Bellows.*) Mama! Chizitere!

(*Enter* NNEBUOGOR, CHIZITERE *and* VALERIA *in a rush.*)

NNEBUOGOR: What is it, Nwandu?

NWANDU: (*Pointing to* VALERIA.) Is she not pregnant?

NNEBUOGOR: (*Walks up to* VALERIA *and starts touching her face and breast, checking to confirm if she's pregnant.*) *Chineke*! You're pregnant.

CHIZITERE: (*Excited and relieved.*) Ah, let me go and call Afamdi. He and his people can come and see Uncle now. (*Exit.*)

NWANDU: Onochie, how did you know that Valeria is pregnant?

(ONOCHIE *is quiet.*) Mama has an eye for these things and she doesn't know. Onochie, what have you done?

ONOCHIE: (*Unconcerned.*) Don't ask me. Ask Valeria.

NWANDU: Mama, please, ask Valeria who put that thing in her womb.

NNEBUOGOR: Nwandu, it's not necessary for us to know who did. She is your father's wife. The child belongs to him.

VALERIA: (*Smiling, to* NWANDU.) If your cornfield is far from your house, the birds will eat your corn.

NWANDU: (*Sudden outburst.*) Onochie, did you do this?

ONOCHIE: (*Trying to calm her.*) This is not what we'll make noise about. All of you blamed me for not being able to father a child. So why point fingers at me now?

NWANDU: (*Grabbing* ONOCHIE *on the hip of his trousers.*) You made a caricature of me in your house and now you've come to mine to make me a laughing stock.

NNEBUOGOR: (*Moving closer to* NWANDU *to stop her.*) Leave him alone, Nwandu. (VALERIA *joins* NNEBUOGOR *to stop* NWANDU.)

NWANDU: (*Still agitated.*) No, Mama. I will kill this man here and now.

VALERIA: (*Holding* NWANDU *by her blouse.*) No! You will not kill my child's biological father.

NNEBUOGOR: Shut up, Valeria. Go and sit down before you hurt that baby in your belly.

VALERIA: I will not.

NWANDU: (*To* VALERIA.) Okay! You've snatched my father from my mother. Now you've taken my husband, too.

(*She leaves* ONOCHIE *and holds* VALERIA *by her blouse.* ONOCHIE *now tries to pull her away from* VALERIA.)

VALERIA: He begged you for over two months and you refused to give him a chance.

NNEBUOGOR: (*Helpless.*) All of you stop this nonsense!

NWANDU: (*Heatedly*.) No, Mama. Two of them, they must kill me. You want to marry two husbands, only you. We must all die here today or my name is not Nwandu.

(*Slow fade*.)

– CURTAIN –

Kraftgriots

Also in the series (DRAMA) *(continued)*

Emmanuel Emasealu (ed.) *The CRAB Plays I* (2008)
Emmanuel Emasealu (ed.) *The CRAB Plays II* (2008)
Richard Ovuorho: *Reaping the Whirlwind* (2008)
Niyi Adebanjo: *Two Plays: A Market of Betrayals & A Monologue on the Dunghill* (2008)
Chris Anyokwu: *Homecoming* (2008)
Sam Ukala: *Two Plays* (2008)
Ahmed Yerima: *Akuabata* (2008)
Kayode Animasaun: *Sand-eating Dog* (2008)
Ahmed Yerima: *Tuti* (2008)
Ahmed Yerima: *Mojagbe* (2009)
Ahmed Yerima: *The Ife Quartet* (2009)
Peter Omoko: *Battles of Pleasure* (2009)
'Muyiwa Ojo: *Memoirs of a Lunatic* (2009)
John Iwuh: *Spellbound* (2009)
Osita C. Ezenwanebe: *Dawn of Full Moon* (2009)
Ahmed Yerima: *Dami's Cross & Atika's Well* (2009)
Osita C. Ezenwanebe: *Giddy Festival* (2009)
Ahmed Yerima: *Little Drops ...* (2009)
Arnold Udoka: *Long Walk to a Dream* (2009), winner, 2010 ANA/NDDC J.P. Clark drama prize
Arnold Udoka: *Inyene: A Dance Drama* (2009)
Chris Anyokwu: *Termites* (2010)
Julie Okoh: *A Haunting Past* (2010)
Arnold Udoka: *Mbarra: A Dance Drama* (2010)
Chukwuma Anyanwu: *Another Weekend, Gone!* (2010)
Oluseyi Adigun: *Omo Humuani: Abubaka Olusola Saraki, Royal Knight of Kwara* (2010)
Eni Jologho Umuko: *The Scent of Crude Oil* (2010)
Olu Obafemi: *Ogidi Mandate* (2010), winner, 2011 ANA/NDDC J.P. Clark drama prize
Ahmed Yerima: *Ajagunmale* (2010)
Ben Binebai: *Drums of the Delta* (2010)
'Diran Ademiju-Bepo: *Rape of the Last Sultan* (2010)
Chris Iyimoga: *Son of a Chief* (2010)
Arnold Udoka: *Rainbow Over the Niger & Nigeriana* (2010)
Julie Okoh: *Our Wife Forever* (2010)
Barclays Ayakoroma: *A Matter of Honour* (2010)
Barclays Ayakoroma: *Dance on His Grave* (2010)

Isiaka Aliagan: *Olubu* (2010)
Emmanuel Emasealu: *Nerves* (2011)
Osita Ezenwanebe: *Adaugo* (2011)
Osita Ezenwanebe: *Daring Destiny* (2011)
Ahmed Yerima: *No Pennies for Mama* (2011)
Ahmed Yerima: *Mu'adhin's Call* (2011)
Barclays Ayakoroma: *A Chance to Survive and Other Plays* (2011)
Barclays Ayakoroma: *Castles in the Air* (2011)
Arnold Udoka: *Akon* (2011)
Arnold Udoka: *Still Another Night* (2011)
Sunnie Ododo: *Hard Choice* (2011)
Sam Ukala: *Akpakaland and Other Plays* (2011)
Greg Mbajiorgu: *Wake Up Everyone!* (2011)
Ahmed Yerima: *Three Plays* (2011)
Ahmed Yerima: *Igatibi* (2012)
Esanmabeke Opuofeni: *Song of the Gods* (2012)
Karo Okokoh: *Teardrops of the Gods* (2012)
Esanmabeke Opuofeni: *The Burning House* (2012)
Dan Omatsola: *Olukume* (2012)
Alex Roy-Omoni: *Morontonu* (2012)
Chinyere G. Okafor: *New Toyi-Toyi* (2012)
Greg Mbajiorgu: *The Prime Minister's Son* (2012)
Karo Okokoh: *Sunset So Soon* (2012)
Sunnie Ododo: *Two Liberetti: To Return from the Void & Vanishing Vapour* (2012)
Gabriel B. Egbe: *Emani* (2012)
Shehu Sani: *When Clerics Kill* (2013)
Ahmed Yerima: *Tafida & Other Plays* (2013)
Osita Ezenwanebe: *Shadows on Arrival* (2013)
Praise C. Daniel-Inim: *Married But Single and Other plays* (2013)
Bosede Ademilua-Afolayan: *Look Back in Gratitude* (2013)
Greg Mbajiorgu: *Beyond the Golden Prize* (2013)
Ahmed Yerima: *Heart of Stone* (2013)
Julie Okoh: *Marriage Coup* (2013)
Praise C. Daniel-Inim: *Deacon Dick* (2013)
Wale Odebade: *Ariyowanye (The Uneasy Head)* (2013)
Soji Cole: *Maybe Tomorrow* (2013) winner, ANA NDDC/J.P. Clark drama prize, 2014
Wunmi Raji: *Another Life* (2013)
Sam Ukala: *Iredi War: A Folkscript* (2014), winner, The Nigeria Prize for Literature, 2014
Bashiru Akande Lasisi: *The First Fight* (2014)
Angus Chukwuka: *The Wedding* (2014)
Prince Ib' Oriaku: *Legend of the Kings* (2014)

Denja Abdullahi: *Death and the King's Grey Hair & Other Plays* (2014)
Walse Tyoden: *Hunting Sekyen* (2014)
Ahmed Yerima: *Orisa Ibeji* (2014)
Julie Okoh: *A Cry for Democracy* (2014)
Chris Anyokwu: *Bloodlines and Other Plays* (2014)
Titus Ohwonohwo: *Edacious Potentate* (2014)
Pius Osuntoyinbo: *Before the Stroke of Noon* (2015)
Bosede Ademilua-Afolayan: *Once Upon an Elephant* (2015)
Dickson Ekhaguere: *Unstable* (2015)
Isiaka Aliagan: *Ogu Umunwanyi* (2015)
Chukwuma Anyanwu: *Two Plays* (2015)
Ahmed Yerima: *Collected Plays I* (2015)
Dimabo Oruama: *The Return of the Golden Sword* (2015)
'Muyiwa Ojo: *Half a Bag of Lies* (2015)
Chidubem Iweka: *August Inmates* (2015)
Ahmed Yerima: *Collected Plays II* (2015)
Ademakinwa Adebisi: *Below the Belt* (2015)
Broderick Esanmabeke Opuofeni: *A Tower of Babel* (2015)
Ameh P. Egwaba: *Love Potion* (2015)
Barclays Ayakoroma: *A Scar for Life* (2015)
Barclays Ayakoroma: *Once Upon a Dream* (2015)
Ahmed Yerima: *Abobaku* (2015)
Doris Ngozi Utuke: *Blood for Love* (2016)